Astrology for Beginners

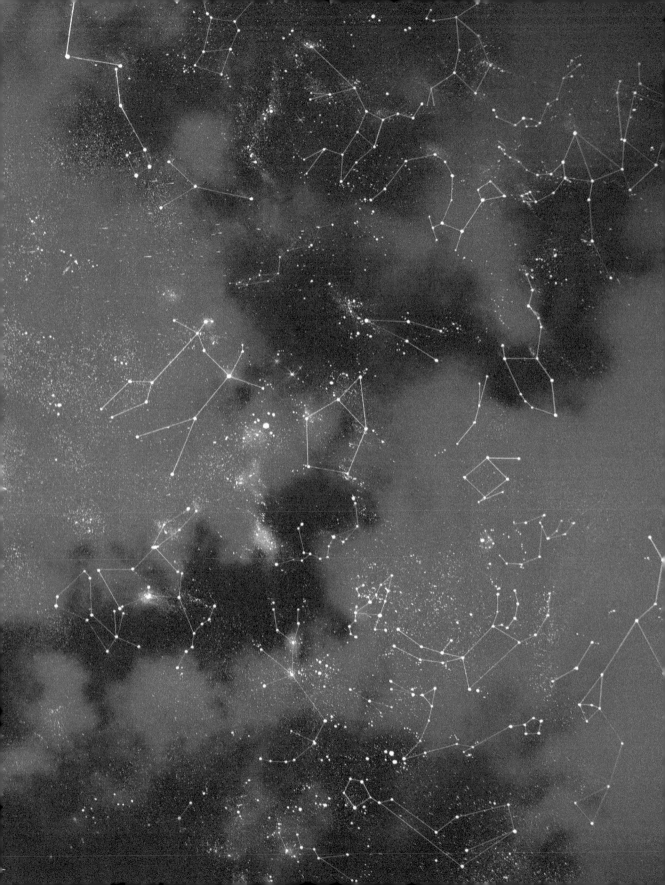

Astrology
for Beginners

A Road Map to Understanding the Language of the Stars

April Pfender

ROCKRIDGE
PRESS

Copyright © 2022 by Rockridge Press

First Rockridge Press trade paperback edition 2022

Rockridge Press and the Rockridge Press logo are trademarks or registered trademarks of Callisto Media Inc. and/or its affiliates in the United States and other countries and may not be used without written permission.

For general information on our other products and services, please contact our Customer Care Department within the United States at (866) 744-2665, or outside the United States at (510) 253-0500.

Paperback ISBN: 978-1-63878-466-1
eBook ISBN: 978-1-63878-789-1

Manufactured in the United States of America

Interior and Cover Designer: Jake Flaherty
Art Producer: Sue Bischofberger
Editor: Chloe Moffett
Production Editor: Ellina Litmanovich
Production Manager: Riley Hoffman

Illustrations used under license from shutterstock.com and iStockphoto.com

Author photo courtesy of Unplug Meditation

10 9 8 7 6 5 4 3 2 1 0

For William, the sun to my moon.
And to my little starlights: Amelia, Lydia, Josh, and Skyla.

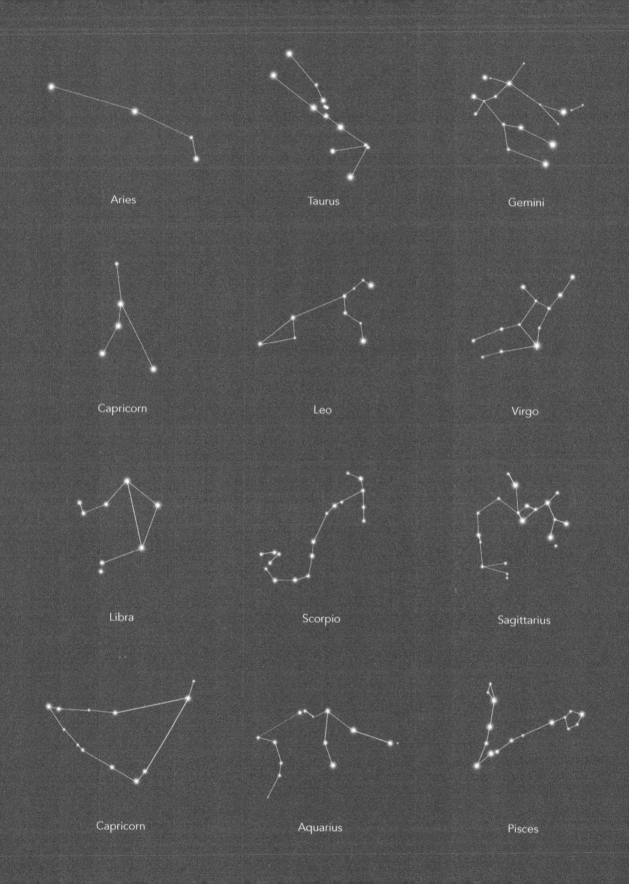

Aries

Taurus

Gemini

Capricorn

Leo

Virgo

Libra

Scorpio

Sagittarius

Capricorn

Aquarius

Pisces

Contents

Introduction

In an ever-evolving world, there is a constant search for answers to free the mind and discover the self. While astrology may not be "the answer," it poses the questions that fuel the journey of self-discovery. The skies provide guidance and encouragement for us along the path of self-inquiry. The planets provide a cosmic blueprint of destiny, and the constellations tell ancient stories of a connection to nature. Humanity was born of stardust, and celestial origins help trace your own incredible origins and set you up to live within the template of your own highest expression. If you have curiosity and a willing heart, astrology can open new doors to your soul. You can get started working with the simple concepts presented in this book right away and see for yourself how astrology can work to enhance your life in every way. It is through the astrological lens that you can build awareness and learn to integrate many of your big (and often challenging) life lessons.

Chances are that if you are reading this book, you have been drawn to healing in your life at a time when you most needed it. You may be experiencing this call even now. I have also been there, searching for answers in the dark. One of the most powerful, life-changing moments for me was discovering astrology. It helped me understand my own behaviors, ways of thinking, and choices. Exploring the planets, placements, signs, and houses in my chart helped me understand energy in ways I hadn't thought about before. I began to recognize the interconnectedness of all life, and I was amazed at the self-reflections this inspired within me. I learned fast, and I grew.

Astrology is something I consider to be a foundational healing tool, and I enjoy incorporating it into my healings for my clients' journeys as well as in my personal lifestyle. As a Reiki master teacher, it is incredibly beneficial to know someone's chart when I'm first starting to work with them. This knowledge helps me fill in the blanks and assists me as we explore a person's physical, mental, emotional, and spiritual development. From looking at someone's birth chart, I can bring objective under-standing to the cycles of behavior they are apt to create so they can make meaningful changes that can help improve their lives. I use astrology to help me track cosmic movement, and I use lunar cycles to plan events and my garden's grow cycles. There are so many practical applications and directions you can go once you make yourself open to the insight astrology provides. Think of this journey as a cosmic remembrance, inching you closer to greater awareness and higher consciousness.

With this book, anyone can learn to integrate basic concepts of astrology into their daily life. Whether you are a student, teacher, or someone keen on learning for yourself, this book's teachings will spell out the basics for you so you can start working with the material right away.

As you begin to wade through the material and flex your astrology muscles, remember that astrology is an entire life journey, and your focus in this book is on foundational elements to get you up and on your feet. It is my hope that the material presented in this book will help you relate in a deeper and more profound way to those around you. But while you are learning, hold a gentle reminder for yourself to take it one step at a time to best integrate the material. There is often a tendency to move at warp speed in this modern world, and that pace is simply not beneficial when immersing yourself in such large topics. Proceed gently and share the material with other souls who might be interested. You might be surprised at how much you already know.

How to Use This Book

et yourself up for success by setting aside protected time to practice whenever you can. For example, carve out time just for astrology on the weekends or during a lunch break. Consistent practice and time spent integrating the material is the easiest way to learn something new. Your knowledge of astrology will build as you experiment and play with the various elements of the zodiac. It's fun, but remember to proceed at a pace that you are comfortable with.

This guide will provide you with foundational information and basic knowledge that you can use to approach astrology with confidence. There are three parts: the first covers an introduction to astrology (think of this as Astro 101), the second is the key components to astrology (Astro 202), and the third contains practical applications with examples. You'll also find a Q&A at the back of the book for quick answers to some common questions from those new to astrology. This guide is designed with the beginner in mind, but it also holds value for those who are brushing up or building upon a basic practice. You'll be provided with key components of the zodiac and guidance for how you can apply the knowledge to interpret birth charts for yourself and your friends. You will want to pull a copy of your birth chart, which will be covered in a later chapter, so get your natal details ready.

With knowledge comes power, and you'll find you're soon able to navigate many different areas of your life with more awareness and understanding. Enjoy the journey as you play with putting what you are learning into practice. Read what you are called to in the moment and take in small bits at a time. Astrology can be fascinating and intriguing, so I wish you many blessings on this enthralling adventure ahead!

Part 1

AN INTRODUCTION TO ASTROLOGY

Astrology is not a system of absolutes. It is a complex and comprehensive method to understanding humans in the context of an intelligent Universe. If anything, the aim is to encourage interpretation and pose questions, rather than telling you who you are. The study of the stars, known as astronomy, goes back thousands of years. Constellations, or groups of stars, created a star map, which helped provide guidance for sailors and the developing civilizations around the world as humanity began to root themselves in solar growth cycles for sustainable living. Life began to thrive on the planet and cosmic origins were woven into the blueprint of humanity's evolution.

This section will explore astrology and how it evolved to become a tool that can be used in everyday life. You'll also learn about the different systems and schools of thought that brought humanity to the doorstep of modern astrology. In addition, you'll be presented with some common myths and misconceptions as well as the many benefits of astrology and how it can enhance your life. Let's get started!

CHAPTER ONE

Astrology 101

strology is a lifelong practice, and this book holds important keys to unlocking the mystery of your own psychological tendencies as well as those of your nearest and dearest in life, your partners, friends, and family members. In the following chapters, you'll learn to begin to map out what is essentially the DNA of the Universe, starting with the building blocks and origin story, which will help you understand what exactly astrology is and what it is not.

Use this book as a road map and come back to various themes to brush up anytime. With this gift comes an ethical responsibility. You can dramatically transform your relationship to yourself as well as the ones closest to you. The more intently you engage with the wisdom on these pages, the more you'll get out of using astrology as a working practice in your life. Committing yourself to learning the essential principles and core tenets of astrology can pay off big time and change your life for good. Let's dive in; the rest will be revealed along the path.

Defining Astrology

Astrology is the study of interpreting the stars, celestial bodies, and planets and how they influence your life. By examining your zodiac, or the wheel representing the placements of the planets and stars at the time of your birth, astrologers can explore the relative influence of these celestial bodies and observe the various dynamics at play within your natal chart. These details can illuminate behaviors, patterns, and potentials, as well as the light (strengths) and shadow (weaknesses) that manifest in an individual's lifetime.

There is no one way to perform a reading of someone's personal astrology (including your own), and this nuance lends to the delight of bringing your personal intuition and insight into the mix. Astrology developed from astronomy, and although astrology is not accredited fully by modern science, I like to think of this craft as a romantic art form, engaging the cosmos in a dance of spiritual connection and tradition. You simply can't quantify some of the aspects your chart is bound to bring up, and that adds to the magic and mystery of it all.

What Astrology Isn't

Though some skeptics are quick to discredit astrology, this practice certainly isn't pseudoscience or just a fad. It has gained popularity in recent years as the quest for knowing oneself grows brighter against the background of an increasingly complex world. Astrology helps you see yourself clearly and encourages you to explore self-inquiry, in lieu of predicting your future or forecasting a specific destiny. Rather than an indicator of personality, love compatibility, or career path, astrology is used to explore new ways of thinking through the questions it poses. Many people also find the study of astrology beneficial due to it being a nonsecular practice that doesn't rely on religion or witchcraft.

Astrology's Origin Story

Astrology has been around for millennia. Ancient cultures dating back more than twenty-five thousand years have built large agriculturally advanced civilizations, temples, sacred sites, and systems based around the perceived movement of stars in the sky. Many stories helped identify the constellations, which inform the modern zodiac themes. The Inca, Maya, and Aztecs, along with many other indigenous cultures, established calendar systems for plotting seasonal changes. As time progressed, a formal calendar developed across Babylon, Greece, Rome, China, India, and Mesoamerica around three thousand years ago, which helped standardize cycles and patterns.

Astrology has evolved over time, and quite rapidly transformed in the past hundred years. One of the key figures to note in astrology's history is Ptolemy (second century CE), who wrote *Tetrabiblos* ("Four Books"), a key astrological text known to bring astrology into academic respectability. It is one of the earliest known writings to put a philosophical slant on astrology. With the onset of physics and astronomy in the fifteenth century, Galileo Galilei popularized the study of the stars with the use of a telescope. In fact, astronomy and astrology were once thought to go hand in hand but diverged during the seventeenth to nineteenth centuries. Alan Leo published the undisputed source of self-instruction for astrology in the early 1900s, catapulting him to fame as "the father of modern astrology." In the 1960s, Carl Jung further explored the theme of astrology, incorporating it into his psychological work and writings. Then, in the late 1970s, Dane Rudhyar coined the term *humanistic astrology,* helping pioneer the practice known today.

The Different Astrology Systems

There are multiple systems to describe astrology, and this book will focus on the tropical zodiac, which is most common in the modern Western world. The system is based on the relationship of the earth and the sun and the resulting seasons. Your chart or horoscope is created from a few vital elements, including your date, time, and place of birth. Yet it is not the stars that move through the sky that provide the constellations, that itself is an illusion. In fact, it is the movement and axis of the earth that creates the perspective of the stars and the planets that are most used today.

Ancient civilizations such as the Egyptians and Maya centered their cultures around what is known as sidereal astrology. Within this system, many branches spread and evolved to be completely independent and unique, such as the Vedic system of astrology, which uses sidereal astrology. Sidereal astrology is based on the position of the sun in relation to the constellations. As such, it is mapped to fixed stars. It's why your sun sign might be different in tropical and Vedic astrology. All placements of planets and celestial bodies help define your overarching habits, traits, tendencies, and behaviors, so whichever one you explore is entirely up to you.

Astrology in Our Modern World

In the late nineteenth century, a resurgence began, rocking the astrology world. Alan Leo is primarily credited with renewing interest in the craft by developing an esoteric approach, which combined spirituality with theosophy. Theosophy aims to connect the concept of source or Universal energy with mystical insights. Leo introduced reincarnation and karma into his work, which ushered in a movement away from event-oriented astrology and put the focus more on character analysis with a psychology spin. Another theosophist, Dane Rudhyar, was also leading the movement to a more psychological approach. Though heavily influenced by Eastern philosophies and work by Carl Jung, this work comprises much of the basis of modern astrology. Some ancient and predictive systems, such as the Mayan calendar, are currently making a comeback among younger astrologers due to these systems' ability to withstand the test of time through the centuries.

Constellations and groupings of stars remain constant, but how they are used within astrology has changed over time. Most ancient astrological texts were quite different from the daily horoscopes seen today. From its early roots, astrology has been a tool used to guide people around the world and to connect with the natural world. It later fell into groupings alongside mathematics, physics, astronomy, and the medical world. Finally, in its current evolution, it stands on its own as a popular art form, grounded in tradition. Much more than entertainment, astrology helps souls find their way by shining a light on the psychology of the human mind and heart.

ARCHETYPES IN THE ZODIAC

Each planet and house in your chart represents an archetype, or thematic Universal principle. These are the guiding forces behind your natal chart, and you should pay attention to them when reading your chart. The archetypes are like characters in the drama of your life, which are all part of you. They combine and interact, like voices within, each with a gift to share. Planets may also present challenges for you, which account for much of the differences of temperament between individuals. Your chart is filled with symbolism and layered meaning if you look closely.

These archetypes were developed long before Carl Jung's primary work on the matter began to surface in the 1960s. His work presented twelve main archetypes (Ruler, Artist, Sage, Innocent, Explorer, Rebel, Hero, Magician, Jester, Everyman, Lover, and Caregiver), which we see reflected in modern zodiac signs and planetary energies today. The planetary names are based on the Roman and Greek pantheons, which are named after ancient gods, goddesses, and mythical creatures. Personal forces in the planets are symbolized by the sun, the moon, Mercury, Venus, Mars, Jupiter, and Saturn while transpersonal or outside forces are symbolized by Uranus, Neptune, and Pluto.

Myths and Misconceptions

Astrology is a highly complicated subject to master. It often represents a lifetime of work to fully understand a horoscope chart inside out and be able to read for others in an accurate and accessible way. Luckily for you, the simple foundational items are presented within this book. There are also many free online resources. At the touch of a button, you can receive your current transits and jump to your own conclusions about what timing and occurrences mean for your life. However, because interpretations can fail and astrologers can be flat-out wrong at times, many people have misgivings about astrology. Instead of placing blame on astrology as a practice, it's good to know a few simple rules before starting your journey. This will help clear up any misconceptions you may have before you begin so that you get started on the right foot.

Your Astrology Is More than Just Your Sun Sign

While your sun sign represents your core outward-facing qualities, your horoscope comprises the planetary placements within the houses of the zodiac wheel. The differences in charts provide for depth; it's one of the reasons you don't resonate with every horoscope or astrological forecast for your primary sign. While it may be a stretch to remember all your planetary placements, it's much easier to remember the Big Three, which will be introduced in chapter 2. Think about the concepts of the archetypes Carl Jung developed. Each planet governs an archetypal or guiding facet within houses of the zodiac. Every single aspect of your birth chart along with the experiences you've had throughout life are what create astrological meaning and impact.

Astrology Is Not All About Predictions

Astrology is not a Magic 8 Ball. Astrology as fortune-telling somehow became popularized when newspapers were publishing one-size-fits-all horoscopes. But just as no horoscope can be inclusive of billions of people simply by sun sign alone, forecasts exist only if you're watching for next week's weather. The aim of astrology is to inform you of your patterns and habits so you can become aware and make changes when needed. Astrology is based on thousands of years of observation. While it had its place in history prophesizing seasonal changes and lunar cycles, it's really about information and self-empowerment nowadays. You can get a good idea of someone's tendencies by looking at their chart; just make sure not to judge a book by its cover.

Astrology Alone Will Not Solve All Your Problems

Astrology can make a great addition to your life and help you on your path in many areas. While it is an amazing tool to help you explore your own depths, it shouldn't be what you rely on to *fix* problems in your life. Deep inner understanding will provide for personal development and great change to occur in the background, which can ultimately be a transformative solution to many challenges. Astrology is a key to the greater puzzle of who you really are. Your thoughts, behaviors, and actions greatly influence the way your life turns out. Since you are the creator of your life, use this responsibility wisely.

How Much of My Life Is Fate vs. Free Will?

We always have a choice. How you show up in the world is purely up to you. There are a multitude of ways in which your astrology can play out in your lifetime, with infinite timelines, mile markers, and scenarios. You have the choice to evolve past your own limitations through your pure will. Signs, planets, progressions, and transits will show you what you are working with, but they won't show you what you are going to choose to do with that. There are so many ways your horoscope can work for you, so believing in any one destiny feels restrictive. Life is about the journey rather than the destination. Enjoy the journey with intention and you'll reap the rewards.

The Benefits of Studying Astrology

There are a multitude of benefits that come from learning and understanding astrology.

Oftentimes life presents edges and boundaries, and the need for self-inquiry and betterment becomes apparent. Astrology can bring understanding of your own experiences into sharper focus, by offering a new angle from which to view them. It allows you an objective view of your own character and a model for understanding the people in your life. As your inner awareness develops, you can transform your life from the inside out. Not only can astrology provide you a stronger sense of connection to your purpose, but you can also use it as a lifelong tool to grow mentally, physically, spiritually, and emotionally.

Open Yourself Up to New Ideas and Perspectives

There's nothing inherently wrong with routine, but unless you step out of your comfort zone and begin to open yourself up to new ideas, you may find yourself rejecting opportunities for solutions in your life. Sometimes the best way to get around that stuck feeling is to simply get out of your own way. Trying something new, like an astrology practice, is a great way to open to new ideas and allow new energies to flow. Use it as a tool to open the mystery areas of your life as you explore, enjoy, and share with others.

Build Your Connection with the Universe

Everything you are interested in, including astrology, represents the Universe pointing its finger to guide you in the right direction. When paired with your powerful intention, it is this energy of excitement that can be used to manifest everything you desire in life. When you tap into this emotion, it helps create new pathways where before there were only doors. The Universe requires a bit of trust, so don't be afraid to lean into it. Ultimately, you'll unlock more doors within.

Incorporate a New Healing Modality into Your Life

If you have ever been curious about self-improvement, you'll find that working with your personal zodiac can be an incredibly healing experience. There are so many tools out there that can be used to harness personal energy, bring peace to past timelines, and analyze the psychology of your behaviors and thoughts. Astrology brings these aspects together in one tool kit under a comprehensive umbrella, and you can use it to supercharge all areas of your life. From improving your career alignment to finding a compatible romantic relationship, there's no area left untouched through this ancient and powerful modality.

Understand the People in Your Life

Not only can astrology help you understand why you act the way you do, but it is also a valuable resource for untangling the many relationship webs presented throughout life. The main characters in your life all play a role, some of them more important than others. Some are cherished, while others have been challenging for you. Some relationships you naturally outgrow and others you keep as lifelong treasures. Astrology not only helps you work with your own energy to break free from toxic cycles and patterns, but it also helps you notice these potential loops within your relationships. Once you understand the nature of the relationships around you, you can more easily put an end to blame games and move into acceptance, even within difficult relationships.

Build Resilience through Self-Inquiry

As you cultivate your astrology practice, it will build your inner resources and help you be more prepared for life's challenges. Self-inquiry can help you deconstruct bad habits and systems of limiting beliefs. You'll become stronger and more resilient as your self-compassion grows. The relationships in your life will shift, and, most important, you'll understand yourself in new ways. This can help you overcome blind spots you didn't notice were there in the first place.

THE CHAKRA-ASTROLOGY CONNECTION

As your spiritual awareness grows, your mind-body connection will also grow. Your own cosmic connection is present throughout astrology, woven into its very fabric. It's no surprise that as you journey through the planetary placements of your personal zodiac, you begin to tap into a divine orchestration that guides you. This personal expansion is reflected in your mind-body connection, through your chakras. Your seven main chakras are your crown, third eye, throat, heart, solar plexus, sacral, and root chakras. The seven main chakras are your personal gateways of energy that run along the body (and in some systems, outside of the body, too).

As you work with different aspects of your chart, you'll find that each planet corresponds to a chakra, much like the archetypes corresponding to the planets. The sun and moon are also represented in the celestial lineup, and these all have a place within the energy centers of the body. As you focus on bringing awareness to certain energies or placements in your chart, your chakra system can be activated within your body. These portals, shaped as wheels, are responsible for governing energy moving in and out of the body, body systems, organs, and glands. They also store energy in the form of emotional imprints.

Keeping clear and open chakras is important if you are interested in healing your body, mind, or spirit. As your planetary connection blossoms, you'll see that astrology is a natural key to developing a stronger and more open chakra system.

Embrace the Power of Astrology

It takes time and dedication to fully be comfortable understanding and interpreting the many elements of astrology, but with practice and consistency, it can give you a whole new outlook on life. The goal is to take small steps whenever you can and keep at it. Astrology can bring you back into living your own gifts and bring about a sense of belonging as you build a stronger sense of awareness of the various roles your ego plays. You aren't born into the world knowing how to think, be, or act. You need to learn how to feel and express emotions in healthy ways and how to treat yourself so you can get the most out of life. Think of astrology as an ongoing practice for your own social-emotional education. Astrology is practical learning for building empathy, compassion, forgiveness, trust, creativity, and healthy emotions.

If you are willing and want to change for the better, astrology creates self-actualization as well as joy and satisfaction to those open to receive its gifts. Your intuition led you here, and within the pages of this book, you'll find years of wisdom packed into one small but mighty astrological guide. By embracing the power of astrology, you can increase your happiness and get more of what you want and need out of your life.

Key Takeaways

This chapter covered some basics to get you moving on your personal astrological journey. You are now better equipped to explore the vast subject of astrology and your own relationship to the cosmos. Here's a quick recap:

◆ Astrology has a rich and diverse history, with multiple systems and interpretations. Western (tropical) astrology is used in this book.

◆ The signs, elements, planets, and houses all interact with one another to deliver a big picture of how you relate and respond to the world around you.

◆ There are many benefits to studying astrology, including how to better understand yourself, as well as the relationships in your life. Astrology can improve your relational and interpersonal skills.

◆ Astrology isn't a one-size-fits-all fix. You should take only what resonates and leave the rest. Don't limit yourself, as you build resilience through self-inquiry.

◆ Your personal zodiac is not meant to tell the future. It simply reflects what your potentials could look like and offers a higher perspective to help you as you navigate challenge in your life.

CHAPTER TWO

Prepare for the Astrological Journey Ahead

 s you prepare for the journey ahead, you'll start by reviewing basic elements, like the signs, modalities, elements, and houses, and then look at how these components factor into a birth chart. This book packs a lifetime of information in it, so feel free to set it down, mark pages, highlight, and come back to it as you need to brush up.

Along with creating an encouraging, supportive environment for yourself as you learn, you'll want to set some goals for yourself as you use this book to advance your astrological prowess. This will help you best navigate your own cosmic blueprint. Since there are so many factors involved in a horoscope chart, it will be important to break these down one at a time so that you can easily digest the material and feel confident putting your new knowledge to work. It's time to gather your tools and get ready.

This Book Will Be Your Road Map

Among the many gifts astrology bestows is the ability to release preconceived notions or judgments (of self and others) that may arise within. The ability to surrender and flow with the waves of life can yield profound results. When you walk into the feeling of overwhelm, you only need to take a pause to realize you are but a deep breath away from emotional freedom. Though the concepts and finer details of a birth chart, along with the many intricate components of astrology, can feel clunky at first, you can always bring it back to the basics to extract clarity and guidance.

It's best to use your time wisely, so I suggest setting aside sacred space where you'll be undisturbed. In this space, you can review the information and genuinely *feel* into what is being shared. I recommend finding a place to unpack this material where your spiritual connection feels enhanced and at ease.

If you are new to astrology or already have a basic practice, this book will serve as an all-in-one resource for you. There's no shame in brushing up on your astrological interpretations, and this book organizes it all so you don't have to. Similarly, if you are working with students in a training program, you'll find that the information shared here is in an easy training format. The knowledge shared here aims to narrow your focus and simplify your workload. The best part is that it can be mined for a lifetime of benefits as you hone your laser-like insights and share your gifts with the world.

An Overview of What's Ahead

The elements, modalities, zodiac signs, planets, houses, and your natal chart are the biggest pieces of the puzzle you'll need to build a firm foundation for your astrology practice. This chapter will prepare you as you get ready to expand your knowledge. Feel free to refer to these quick on-the-go definitions as you dive into the material in this book. Knowing how to work with these components and how they interplay with one another will enable you to quickly extract the highlights in a zodiac reading. You'll be more likely to access a complete, nuanced picture, much more than a simple sun sign can tell you. These all contribute to a person's makeup, so by understanding them individually, you'll be one step closer to assembling the pieces as they go together in a reading. Let's take a closer look.

The Four Elements and Three Modalities

The building blocks of the Universe, as well as the zodiac, are the four elements: fire, earth, air, and water. These can also be linked to archetypal representations and are commonly found everywhere in the natural world. There are three signs in the zodiac that fall under each elemental category. Elements can provide an indication of how a person behaves and reacts in situations. The elements can be very telling when it comes to discovering primary traits of an individual. These groupings are further divided into three modalities: cardinal, fixed, and mutable. The modalities indicate the sign's behavioral tendencies. When they are blended together, they give an even clearer picture of a person's general tendencies.

The Twelve Zodiac Signs

The signs represent the psychological *needs* in the zodiac. Most of the planets and celestial bodies move through the constellations of the zodiac along an ecliptic through space, which is an orbital band. In a chart, the signs move around the fixed houses, which gives them the appearance of revolving from our perspective. The zodiac signs always follow the same order as they revolve around a chart, starting in Aries, moving to Taurus, Gemini, Cancer, Leo, Virgo, Libra, Scorpio, Sagittarius, Capricorn, Aquarius, and Pisces. Though you can learn much from a simple sun sign, you can really begin to illuminate a chart by knowing the planetary placements and which houses they fall within.

The Planets

It is commonly said that the planets describe *what* is talked about in a zodiac reading, while the zodiac signs more accurately describe *how* it feels. This explains certain planet-sign combinations and how they interact for better or worse (though no planet is bad, some can present challenges). The planets each rule a sign of the zodiac, and some rule more than one. For all intents and purposes, the sun and moon are considered planetary bodies in these definitions. Therefore, the planets are the sun, the moon, Mercury, Venus, Mars, Jupiter, Saturn, Neptune, Uranus, and Pluto. You can think of each planet as part of your psyche, which is contained within the whole. The celestial bodies are grouped into personal planets and outer planets, reflecting how they are active and which roles they play in your life.

The Twelve Houses

The houses represent the *where* area in life in which the planet and signs are active. These life-activity areas are divided into twelve, and they cover all cross sections of your life. The first six segments deal with your personal affairs, like home life, money, and health, while the last six segments deal with things outside the self— partners, community, opportunities, and idealism. How many planets fall in each house within your zodiac will denote how much activity that house sees and where your focus in life exists. Each house represents a slice of the pie, and they are fixed in a chart, which means that they stay in the same position while the signs revolve around them counterclockwise.

Your Natal Chart

Your birth chart is also known as your natal chart. It includes the location, date, and exact time of birth. You can punch in your details on free websites and apps for a simple report. I personally really like Co-Star, Time Passages, and Astro.com for easy go-to charts. I suggest printing out your chart so you can take notes on the page and make things easy for yourself. Details are often available on long-form birth certificates or hospital records, but if you don't have access to that information, just enter 12:00 p.m. This will ensure most of the information is as close as possible. You won't be able to get the ascending (rising) sign, and your moon sign may not be correct, but it will be close.

Aspects

The planets and other celestial bodies are connected through various aspects. Aspects are the angles that are made between the bodies throughout a chart. As angles, these are measured in degrees and refer to the distance between points in the horoscope. Aspects help create the full picture of an astrology chart because they help fill in the blanks and connect disparate elements to create a cohesive story. Aspects can be highly complex, and though you'll notice the lines connecting celestial bodies, it's not as important to pay attention to these when you are first starting to read a chart. In general, aspects can be positive or negative, like night and day, within a chart. They can also form conjunctions, or intersections where energies meet. These can be powerful places of focus within a chart, so make note of them as they come up.

CREATE A SACRED SPACE FOR SUPPORT

Most practitioners of the sacred arts find it helpful to set up a supportive environment when starting a new practice, such as astrology. This space should be a quiet zone, free from distractions. It should foster calming and positive energies. As you settle in comfortably to begin your reading practice, you want to feel inspired and surrounded by spaciousness. Give yourself enough time without feeling rushed. Light a candle and place your favorite crystal, or any object that you use for meditation, around you. It may also help you to clear the area first of any clutter, then smudge the space with sage or palo santo. The smoke from these dried herbs can help clear any negative ions and energies from a space.

Spending a few moments getting centered by clearing your breath can help you focus your intentions and drop into an intuitive space so you can really open up. Ground your practice after you are done with your reading by clearing the room again and spending a few moments in peace and gratitude before moving on to the rest of your day. Over time, cultivating a mindful sacred space will really make a difference.

Astrology Can Support Your Personal Growth

Once you start working with astrology, you'll notice that it can provide insights, lessons, and opportunities for personal growth in many areas of your life. From creativity to career, communication to conflict, and friendship to romance, many of the things you care most about are represented through astrology. You can go as deep as you need or want to within each area to completely heal shadows and wounding or bring extra attention to what's already working for you in your life. I think you'll find that in a short period of time, your views can shift, and you'll be opening up on new levels to ultimately step into the person you are becoming, the very best version of you.

Nurture Self-Reflection and Self-Discovery

It is said that self-trust is cultivated by inner alignment. The more you create and follow positive experiences, the more your body and mind will follow suit. You begin to trust yourself. Your thoughts and actions will be well informed because you are opening up to the information that comes from inner knowledge. Self-discovery is one of the greatest pursuits you can undertake in this lifetime, and astrology can provide that. Time spent in deep self-reflection with the information you receive through your horoscope might bring up even more questions for you. Self-study is valuable because oftentimes there is so much to unpack in one lifetime. So do yourself a favor and give yourself plenty of time and space to do this important work.

Explore Who You Truly Are

Through the process of self-inquiry, you may meet some resistance. This will require wholehearted focus and discipline to work through. However, practicing astrology can be quite empowering. As you deepen your relationship with the material in this book, you'll begin to unlock codes to your human potential. You are on a path of awakening and discovering who you really are, which is something both precious and priceless. Committing to knowing your true nature is a devotion to your own essence. This is who you are beyond the role you play, the possessions you own, your success and failures, and even how others define you. Who you truly are is a soul having a beautiful human experience, and astrology can help illuminate the way.

Find Guidance Through Life's Challenges

Tapping into astrology can give you guidance on the next steps to take. Challenges are a natural part of life, and you can either allow them to get the best of you or choose to move through them as gracefully as possible. By closely examining your own light and shadow within each realm or house, you'll start to uncover new ways of navigating difficulties on your own terms. For example, if you are experiencing issues around finances, you can peek into your second house in your chart, which is all about value, money, and possessions, to find out how to best optimize your energies. The knowledge you discover can signal how you attract or repel money, which you can use to your advantage.

Measure Your Compatibility with Friends, Family, and Partners

Using astrology can provide accurate measurements of your emotionality, personality, ideals, strengths, and weaknesses, as well as those of your friends, family, and partners. You can gain valuable insights about the relationship between two people and all the potentials that exist within the dynamic by glancing at your charts. You'll want to grab natal details for a full chart for this one. You can measure this by looking at your chart synastry, which details all the compatible and challenging aspects of two full charts, or a composite chart, which is made by overlapping the two charts and seeing the commonalities between them. Many sites (like Co-Star) will create a composite for you, or you can pay for this service as an extra fee since these can be more complicated.

Plan for the Future

Ancient cultures used the sun to gauge the agricultural cycles according to the seasons. But did you know that you can use astrology to plan for your future? Tracking and planning the lunar (moon) cycles, retrograde cycles (discussed later in this book), and planetary transits can help you chart your course ahead. In fact, you can identify these cycles as far ahead of time as you'd like to make sure you have plenty of time to prepare. For example, you might want to plan a big life event, like a wedding or a move, outside of a retrograde season, or you can schedule some intention setting for the next new moon.

Cosmic Support

As you commit to using astrology in an aligned way, you'll find much spiritual expansion is created. By focusing on a practice filled with integrity and drawing meaning from the Divine, you will be able to feel cosmic support for all your thoughts, actions, and behaviors. As you step into your own creatorship by taking responsibility within your personal chart, you'll get a sense of magnification of your Universal connection and the force that drives it into being. You hold the capacity to evolve beyond your current experience through a greater, more unified expression. Astrology is a vehicle to help take you there by expanding your psychological and spiritual operating systems.

Set Some Goals for Using this Book

It's helpful to set your intentions ahead of time when you are developing a new practice. Set aside some time to work out your personal goal setting beforehand if possible. When you set goals for yourself, it gives you something to work toward and can help motivate you along your path. By clarifying the direction you'd like your practice to take early on, you'll be able to clearly focus on building your new habits, one at a time.

For example, your goals might be to improve your personal relationships or to plan for future business challenges. In this way, you'll be able to focus directly on how you need astrology to work for you. Since there is so much information in astrology, the best results are the ones that contain a focused lens on the exact issue requiring a solution. By holding yourself accountable with some way to measure your results, you'll ensure you stay inspired and motivated, and you'll be more likely to stay with your practice.

WHAT DOES IT MEAN IF I'M BORN ON A CUSP?

If you are born on a cusp, you are straddling the line between two distinct signs. This phenomenon creates a blended personality, which holds the properties of both signs. *Cusp*, from the Latin word for spear or point, is a line separating two consecutive signs in the zodiac. The term refers to a person whose birthday falls on the point of transition between the end of one zodiac sign and the start of another.

For example, if you were born on March 20, your sun sign is technically Pisces, but this is a point where the sun is beginning to move into Aries. For the cusp individual, this means you'll exhibit tendencies of a Piscean-Aries blend. Sometimes you'll be dreamy and serene, and other times you'll feel fiery and hot-tempered.

This is also true of other cusp blends. Some people consider three days before the official sign change and three days after the new zodiac sign to be the cusp. You can feel into what's right for your reading, but it's good to glance at both zodiac signs if the birthdate you are working with falls on the day before, day of, or day after a sun transits signs.

Gather Your Tools

As the time draws near for you to engage in astrology in a meaningful way, you'll want to spend some time gathering your tools. You are only as strong as the tools in your tool kit, and some of these may take time to pull together, so you'll want to get started early. Once you have your basic components gathered and your sacred space created for practice, you'll be well on your way to setting yourself up for success.

The good news is most of these items are free—the task is simply to educate yourself and apply your newfound knowledge whenever and wherever you can. Remember that a strong practice is just that—a practice! Spend time with these details often (and get into the habit of asking for them up front) to make the most out of your readings.

Your Time, Date, and Place of Birth

The most common question asked in astrology is "What's your sign?" This question is almost always referring to your sun sign. Sometimes it's the only part of your chart you may know. For example, if you aren't sure of your biological birth records or they were not recorded, you'll need to estimate this part. This is probably the biggest key to having extremely accurate information for your reading. Not to worry, you can still understand a few key elements with a simple date of birth. If you are unsure of this information, working with your sun sign is still going to provide some amazing and valuable information for you. However, you will be unable to distill exact moon or rising signs without knowing a specific time and place of birth.

Get Familiar with the Symbols

The symbols of the zodiac are called glyphs. These are small icons that represent the planets, celestial bodies, aspects, and signs in a chart. These are often used as shorthand symbols during readings, and many charts (like a zodiac wheel or astro-cartography chart) do not write out the names because it clutters the page and can be too much information to present in one chart. Knowing the symbols in advance will give you an advantage for reading fluently, just as learning the local language will help you navigate your way in a foreign country. Once you learn these, you'll ensure that you won't have to spend time going back and forth looking up each glyph of a chart, which can ultimately save you mountains of time.

The Big Three

The trifecta of your sun, moon, and rising (ascending) signs are often known as the Big Three in astrology. This is an excellent place to start when just beginning to review your personal zodiac or that of a friend. Rather than focusing purely on a sun sign (as with a horoscope in a publication), I encourage you to dig for the information associated with the other signs. Working with the Big Three is a great way to narrow down your reading, which will give you the most impactful information in a short amount of time.

Key Takeaways

It is my hope that you leave this chapter feeling encouraged on your decision to learn about astrology and feel well equipped with some tips to set you up for success on your new endeavors. Although astrology can be complex, you can help your learning journey by preparing well for the next steps ahead. The main highlights from this chapter include:

◆ By creating a calm, nurturing, undisturbed, and sacred space in which to conduct astrology, you'll be setting yourself up to receive the most support.

◆ Your astrology practice can help you on your path of self-inquiry and shed valuable insights into who you truly are. All that's required is a willingness to go deep.

◆ Some of the major components of astrology include houses, signs, elements, modalities, and birth charts.

◆ Being born on a cusp is a common occurrence, happening when a person's birthdate falls on or very close to two signs.

◆ You'll need your birth date, location, and exact time of birth to procure a natal chart with specific sun, moon, and rising signs (the Big Three). If you don't have this, you can apply the information in this book to your main sun sign.

Part 2

THE KEY COMPONENTS
OF ASTROLOGY

Now that we've gone over how to best lay a foundation for the bulk of your astrology practice and set up your astrotools, you can begin to journey at your own pace. You'll be well equipped with your road map, which you'll find in this next section of the book, consisting of the basic components of an astrology practice. To help you along your way, you'll will be presented with greater depth and definition regarding the four elements, three modalities, the twelve zodiac signs and houses, and the planets along with the other included luminary bodies.

Remember that the solar system is a living system that is reflected through each of us internally. The macrocosm, or large picture, is always mirrored in the microcosm, or tiny pieces that make up the whole. Your solar system goes through cycles, possesses yin/yang energies, and holds infinite quantum possibilities. Not only will this next section provide you with a solid, working infrastructure for building your astrology skills, but it will also set you up to be able to interpret parts of your own psyche as you associate each new piece of learning with the Universe at large. Enjoy the journey.

CHAPTER THREE

The Four Elements and Three Modalities

n this chapter, we will explore the basic elements that will form the foundation of your astrological practice. We will look at the primary elements of nature (fire, earth, air, and water) and how they translate to your life. You'll notice that some of these elements are familiar, as you've likely felt their presence in different ways throughout your lifetime.

You will then learn about the modalities (cardinal, fixed, mutable), which are an important part of understanding astrology. The modalities indicate a method of approach or mode of operating in which the signs behave. Once you know and understand how to identify which element and modality your signs fall under, you can gain enormous benefit and insight. Without understanding much else in your chart, but starting with these building blocks, you can create a basic picture of behavior, personality, drives, and ego functions for any chart. Categorizing signs doesn't have to be hard. It can be as simple as starting with what you know. As always, stretch your mind and have fun with it. This is where your journey truly begins.

What Are the Four Elements?

Astrological charts can be complex and difficult to make sense of. To untangle the web without drowning in detail, let's start by examining the four elements, the foundations of astrology and essence of nature itself. The four elements make learning the zodiac fun and easy because if you have no other information but your sun sign, you'll still be able to tell a lot about someone's character by their associated element. The elements are fire, earth, air, and water. Each of these govern three zodiac signs, and each of these represent a quality or characteristic. For example, fire represents spirit, earth embodies physical matter, air equates to the intellect, and water exemplifies emotion.

In approximately 450 BCE, the Greeks came up with a theory that the four elements created all life on this planet. They viewed the elements as original building blocks to the Universe, representing the different aspects of the natural world. Later, Plato added to this theory, and the four elements became a cornerstone to philosophy, physics, mathematics, astronomy, and astrology. The Greeks believed the elements were unchanging in nature and that they were held together or pushed apart by forces of attraction and repulsion. The elements described not only everything found in nature, but also everything found inside oneself.

What Do They Teach You?

Each element, or energy, is reflected within different aspects of you, as you are made up of the entire Universe within you. Your physical body, your emotions, your mind, and your spirit all make up the essence of who you really are. These characteristics inform your personality, tendencies, and attributes. They can help highlight behavioral patterns and assist you in recognizing and accepting these traits within others. As the elements are the building blocks of the natural world, remember that each offers its own medicine and learnings. They should be treated as archetypal themes and explored inside and out so you can extract the inherent intelligence they each hold.

Each of the elements associates with three of the zodiac signs. Therefore, it's possible to experience an additive effect if your particular combination of sun/moon/rising signs contain two or more of the same element. For example, if you have an Aries sun/Leo moon/Leo rising, your Big Three all hold the fire element, which means your dominant expression would be fire forward. If your chart denotes an Aquarius sun/Taurus moon/Virgo rising, your chart contains a more proportionate blend of primary energies and elements (though you are still expressing as earth dominant). You'll want to look elsewhere in your chart to notice different elemental themes that can create more balance, such as your planetary placements. The planetary placements should be able to show you some elemental variance and help you understand more nuanced expressions of yourself.

Fire

The fire signs are Aries, Leo, and Sagittarius, ruling the first, fifth, and ninth houses of the zodiac. Fire is a good place to begin an elemental journey in the zodiac, as Aries kicks off the astrological calendar year. Faces of fire can be found throughout nature through time. For example, the sun, the solar luminary, burns and emits life-giving energies to the planet, giving rise to all other elements as it enables photosynthesis for oxygen, ozone, condensation, and weather. Perhaps one of the most influential, intense, and dominant of the elements, fire is expansive, and a symbol of the Divine light within.

If you've got fire in your chart, especially within your Big Three, you naturally have a forging will and burning determination that goes above and beyond. Go Big or Go Home is your motto, and you have great motivation and initiative. Individuals with a primary fire element tend to bring a fun and enthusiastic approach to their work and life and hold an unparalleled passion for action and excitement. You'll rarely find this bunch sitting on the sidelines, as patience and latency isn't their nature. This group is the stuff leaders are made of, and they want you to know it. Never ones to shy away from confrontation or an opportune chance to shine, fire signs are known to unabashedly bring the heat. Work with the fire element when you are going through times of deep transformation and seeking to reemerge anew.

Earth

Up next in the elemental trek through the zodiac is earth, grounding and nurturing in its essence. The earth signs are Taurus, Virgo, and Capricorn ruling the second, sixth, and tenth houses of the zodiac. Historically, as the stardust from the Big Bang cooled and condensed, atomic particles settled into chunks of rock, eventually forming the planets known today. Earth represents a beautiful balance of all the elements, resulting in a great home. Earth is connected to the solid matter that structures the Universe. Giving form to the physical human body and all of creation, earth is both a conduit and a container for the other elements. This quality is best known for its substantiative and settled nature.

Those with earth-dominant signs in a chart will feel stable and restful in their natural state. Earth signs are typically slow-moving and dependable friends, partners, and coworkers. They are more interested in material luxuries and concerned with beauty and comfort rather than the speed with which they get things done. Earth signs possess a strong inner wisdom, and this group gives meaning to the phrase "Slow and steady wins the race." Like the ground beneath your feet, earth signs offer reliable and enduring relationships to those around them. Pragmatic, thoughtful, and deliberate, there is a gravity to this element that feels strong and secure. Work with the earth element when you're in need of steady, deep-rooted rebalancing.

Water

Flowing full of emotions, the water signs embody some big-wave energies. The water signs are Cancer, Scorpio, and Pisces ruling the fourth, eighth, and twelfth houses of the zodiac. Sensual and sublime, water flows and blesses the creatures and land around it with life-giving gifts. The water element is present in streams, rivers, lakes, oceans, snow, ice, and rain. It is in the morning dew on a blade of grass and the waves upon a shore lapping at your feet. Water signifies purification, fluidity, clarity, and redemption in a spiritual sense. This element creates healing yet holds the power to both destroy and sustain life.

Water signs are often misunderstood, as they carry a depth that mimics the unwavering intensity of fire, yet this depth has no edges. At their core, water signs are penetrating yet calm, cool, and collected. These individuals tend to go one of two ways. They may either be the fast-acting, restless, and busy type or are gentle, peaceful, and tranquil. Either way, water signs possess a sharp intellect and can pivot on a dime if a redirect is necessary. They can be a force to be reckoned with, yet they have a softer side. These types are intuitive and enjoy playing in the nebulous and imaginative dream-world realms. The water element in a chart can indicate a moody demeanor with an underlying sensitivity. Work with the water element to cool off your hot temper or to bring compassion into an area that is lacking.

Air

 Air is the final element in the zodiac, conveying superior intellect, knowledge, and prowess over matters of the mind. The air signs are Gemini, Libra, and Aquarius, ruling the third, seventh, and eleventh houses of the zodiac. Air is all around you, an unseen force that moves the sand upon dunes, leaves on the trees, and wind through your hair. Bringing change with it, this element can be light and airy or breezy and swift. Representing vital breath, air connects the spirit to the mind and body. It is the animating force and primary nutrient that also moves through you, giving life.

Those born under an air sign tend to have curious minds, highly developed communication skills, and lots of initiative. Their ambitious nature often keeps them busy, and their personality is good at making decisions as well as carrying them through. Air signs tend to judge themselves (and others) quite intensely, as they hold particularly high standards. They are known to be the socialites and storytellers of the zodiac and are often excellent networkers because of this. They have plenty of friends to go around and are known to be the friend everyone goes to to help sort out problems because of their advanced abilities of memory and reason. Quick-witted and rational, an air sign doesn't spend too much time languishing in emotions or stuck in a rut as they are far too preoccupied with solving life's many mysteries. Work with the air element when you need to bring momentum and build energy to welcome in new ideas and direction.

THE FIFTH ELEMENT

The four original elements are foundational to learning astrology as well as building your archetypal skills throughout all of life. Early concepts that attempted to explain the nature of the material world was humankind's way of understanding the Universe, but various cosmologies and ancient cultures believe in the existence of five essential elements. In Hinduism, the elements are associated with the five senses, and we see associations with the elements and our own chakra system. Fire, earth, air, and water have a fifth sibling called ether, which was introduced by Aristotle. Later, Plato was credited with the idea of the platonic solids, which are the sacred geometric shapes that the elements are associated with.

If fire, earth, air, and water take up space and create all that is, ether is the glue that holds them all together. It is thought to be all the elements combined. Though it's not represented in astrology along with the other elements, it is regarded by well-known alchemists and philosophers to be *quinta essential*, or the quintessential element that holds the soul or spirit essence. When each of the other elements' symbols are geometrically nested on top of each other, they combine to create ether's symbol, called Solomon's seal. The all-encompassing ether element is associated with the dodecahedron platonic solid, whose twelve sides represent the twelve constellations of the zodiac.

| Fire | Earth | Air | Water | Ether |

What Are the Three Modalities?

Along with the elements, the modalities, or quadruplicities, in astrology can say so much about your personality and can give you important insight on your own expression of energy. The three modalities are cardinal, fixed, and mutable, with each modality connecting to four signs of the zodiac. These classifications describe how you react to different circumstances and how you operate in the world. Known as the modus operandi of the signs, the modalities represent how the signs can move and evolve with time. They describe the mode under which the signs do things and the methods they use in their approach.

Although modalities and elements are both designations in astrology and are both used to categorize the twelve signs, the two are very different. While the elements represent the motivations or qualities of the group, the modalities represent the manner of expression for those qualities. It is interesting to note that each modality contains one sign from each of the four elements and vice versa (each element contains one sign from each of the three modalities). This means that the energies are evenly accounted for across both systems. The mode of a sign also reflects the position of the season in which it's found. The earlier signs of the season are cardinal, the middle are fixed, and end-of-season signs are mutable. If you want to spot someone based on their modality, there are a few telltale signs to look out for, which you'll be introduced to as you explore each modality in the pages to come.

ASTROLOGY AND THE MEDICINE WHEEL

Native American and other Indigenous cultures have used the four elements and four cardinal signs for millennia in a traditional medicine wheel. A medicine wheel can help depict and describe the seasons and movement of the natural world. It's used to help people understand change and move through shifts gracefully. In a medicine wheel, the four cardinal (or primary) directions are represented, along with the four elements. In the Northern Hemisphere, cardinal fire (Aries) kicks off spring equinox, cardinal water (Cancer) ushers in summer solstice, cardinal air (Libra) initiates fall equinox, and cardinal earth (Capricorn) welcomes winter solstice. In the Southern Hemisphere, these are reversed. Though many lineages and cultures have many different interpretations of the wheel, this description is widely used to this day.

These four directions are symbolic of the different stages of life, beginning in the East with birth (fire, initiations) and moving to the South representing youth (water, emotional innocence, purity). The wheel then moves West to adulthood (earth, physical energy), and finally this energy is complete in the North as an elder (air, wisdom). The zodiac is a sacred loop with which you can focus and align your energies. All is connected in the great mandala of life, and all of life's lessons repeat as needed, moving cyclically in an unending ring until the lessons are achieved.

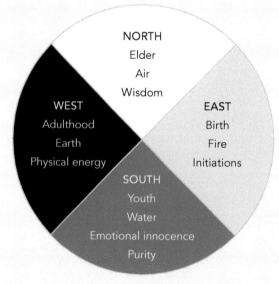

Cardinal

The cardinal signs are Aries, Cancer, Libra, and Capricorn, which fall in the first, fourth, seventh, and tenth houses. These signs open each quadrant of the zodiac as primary, or "first," signs. If an abundance of your planets falls within these houses, your zodiac energy is weighted toward cardinality. Cardinal signs tend to show up in life with initiating energy, always starting new projects and launching into things full force. These types are ambitious, self-motivated, and possess a drive that is unmatched in much of the zodiac, making them natural leaders and achievers. Although these signs are fond of beginning new plans, they do have some trouble following them to completion, as finishing is not their strong suit. Whatever they get involved with, there's always a lot going on. Count on these innovators to be the generators of ideas and first to bring a scheme into motion.

The energy of cardinal signs can come off as a bit domineering and slightly aggressive at first. This is owed to the fact that they love to embrace a zest for life and hold a deep passion for anything they get involved with from the start. If there's a prize for coming in first, cardinal signs are in it to win it. However, they can tend to be so focused on their own endeavors that they sometimes get tunnel vision, but luckily their energetic spirit often redeems them. Count on these visionaries to create things seemingly out of thin air and to be able to execute a plan with determination.

Fixed

The fixed signs are Taurus, Leo, Scorpio, and Aquarius, which fall in the second, fifth, eighth and eleventh houses. These signs show up in the middle of each quadrant of the zodiac, and if an abundance of your planets fall within these houses, your zodiac energy is predominantly fixed. Leave it to the fixed signs to capitalize on cardinal signs' ideas. These are the people who will be running the plans to the finish line. Whereas cardinal energy often begins but rarely ends an intention, fixed signs are the "doers" of the zodiac, accomplishing whatever the plan is by taking care of all the middle details.

Fixed signs are known to be stubborn, but this is one of their valuable characteristics, as they persevere when times get tough. In fact, it's one of their standout qualities. They know how to identify what needs to be done and then put in the elbow grease to make it work. Their main traits can be considered dedication and momentum because it's when they are in the thick of something that their strengths really shine. Steadfast and resolute, these types achieve their objectives with a calm and collected demeanor. The persistence and focus of fixed signs pay off because they always get results. This is part of their personal power. Just don't tell a fixed sign they are wrong, this modality is strong but sensitive. Count your blessings to have fixed signs as your friends. They make the most reliable friends, because you can count on them to always be there for you no matter what.

Mutable

The mutable signs are Gemini, Virgo, Sagittarius, and Pisces, which fall in the third, sixth, ninth, and twelfth houses. These signs show up at the end of each quadrant of the zodiac, and if an abundance of your planets falls within these houses, your zodiac energy is mainly mutable. If the cardinal signs help get things started, and the fixed signs see those tasks through, then the mutable signs are here to fill in the blanks and assist with embracing inevitable change. These signs represent the finality or end of each season, so they are exceptionally good at establishing ending and bringing closure to a situation. They may tend to stray from the main idea a bit and get carried away in their own thoughts, but if you manage to pin this sign down, you'll find they have a crafty solution up their sleeves.

Mutable signs are rather adept at pivoting to accommodate the unexpected challenges and shifts in life, and they do quite well with change. They prefer to conform to the norm, rather than stand out in a crowd, but don't get them wrong, this group is versatile and dynamic. Always the opportunist, a mutable sign finds a way to stretch the resources to make a dream come true and they are flexible enough to flow with whatever is unfolding in the present moment. These individuals are considered to be the accepting shape-shifters of the bunch and whether it's a work project, conversation, or season, with a mutable sign around you can trust that things will be brought to a natural conclusion.

Key Takeaways

This chapter was packed with knowledge about the elements and modalities, and there is still so much more to learn about astrology. With these simple foundations, you'll be on your way to starting your practice in no time. Let's look at some core concepts that were presented in this chapter.

◆ The four elements of astrology are fire, earth, air, and water. These elements make up the building blocks, or qualities, of the solar system and help you understand life on a Universal level.

◆ Each element governs three signs in the zodiac.

◆ The elements in astrology can also be thought of as archetypes, or fundamental aspects that cannot be broken down into any other thing.

◆ The three modalities in astrology are cardinal, fixed, and mutable. These modalities are used to describe how a sign behaves and responds to life.

◆ Each modality governs four signs in the zodiac.

◆ A quick chart to summarize the elements and modalities:

Aries: Cardinal Fire

Taurus: Fixed Earth

Gemini: Mutable Air

Cancer: Cardinal Water

Leo: Fixed Fire

Virgo: Mutable Earth

Libra: Cardinal Air

Scorpio: Fixed Water

Sagittarius: Mutable Fire

Capricorn: Cardinal Earth

Aquarius: Fixed Air

Pisces: Mutable Water

CHAPTER FOUR

The Twelve Zodiac Signs

ow, it's time to dive into the main course of the zodiac by looking at the twelve zodiac signs more closely. This chapter will examine each of the sign's characteristics and traits, why they are important, and what role they play astrologically. You will also explore how each sign has a ruling planet, or luminary, and tends to play out its own energy and dramas.

By 1500 BCE, the Babylonians had already divided the zodiac into twelve equal parts. This was determined by the thirty-day-per-month calendar cycle. The identification and naming of the constellations sprung from myths (The Great Twins, The Scales, The Lion). The Greeks later adopted the constellations into their own pantheon, which is how they are known in modern astrology. Even the word *zodiac* is Greek; it means "sculpted animal figure." Let's take a closer look to find out what exactly the signs are and how they came to be.

What Are the Twelve Zodiac Signs?

In Western astrology, the zodiac is divided into twelve signs, which correspond to the twelve constellations. These star groups are marked by the path the sun travels during a year. It's important to remember that even though the stars appear to move around the earth, the earth is tilted on an axis and constantly revolving around the sun. This gives the perceived appearance of the constellations moving through the skies each night and changing throughout the year with the seasons. Each sign has its own energies, qualities, and attributes, which influence and guide your life. The way you react and respond, the way you think and behave, and the way you feel about things can all be mapped through the signs. Your signs are like an outfit that you wear, or the style in which you interact with the world.

Like all elements in astrology, some zodiac signs blend well together, and some tend to naturally oppose each other. Compatibility should be based on a full picture, including elements, planetary aspects, and houses in which the signs fall under in your birth chart. Looking at a chart is like reading music. You wouldn't just read one note on a page to sing. You must read the whole thing to create a song. Each sign holds two sides: its evolved state (merits) and shadow (detriments). Each sign brings a unique and individual outlook to life. Many of life's interactions may be informed by the signs.

DEGREES IN THE ZODIAC

The astrology wheel is measured by a full 360-degree circle. Each sign within the zodiac, which can be thought of as a slice, is divided into 30 degrees. For example, Aquarius starts at 0 degrees and goes to 29 degrees, followed by Pisces at 0 degrees. You're able to expand upon the meaning behind each planet's placement in a chart through examining which degree it's in.

The different degrees are each represented by a zodiac sign, which means if you've got a planet in this degree, you'll want to add the sign qualities when you're examining that planet. For example, if you have Pisces in Taurus at the eleventh degree, you could add Aquarius qualities when examining that placement. Look at the chart below to get a glimpse of the signs and degrees they pair with or exemplify.

0°	Double whammy! Interpret this as doubling the energy of the zodiac placement.
1°, 13°, 25°	Aries (bold, brave, fast)
2°, 14°, 26°	Taurus (stubborn, material world, stability)
3°, 15°, 27°	Gemini (communication, curiosity)
4°, 16°, 28°	Cancer (home, emotions)
5°, 17°, 29°	Leo (charismatic, leader)
6°, 18°	Virgo (organization, service)
7°, 19°	Libra (harmony, beauty)
8°, 20°	Scorpio (intense, transformation)
9°, 21°	Sagittarius (freedom, travel)
10°, 22°	Capricorn (prestige, hard work)
11°, 23°	Aquarius (humanitarian, technology)
12°, 24°	Pisces (mystical, imagination)

Exploring Your Sun, Moon, and Rising Signs

Though your sun (solar) sign is the most talked-about and commonly referenced sign in your chart, your moon (lunar) and ascendent (rising) signs can each illuminate different aspects for you. Have you ever noticed that two of your Leo friends are nothing alike? By looking at the Big Three in closer detail, you can infer much detail and nuance within a chart.

Your sun sign represents your outward-shining ego or personality. Just like the sun radiates warmth and life-giving light, this portion of your chart is a highlight of who you are at your core. This is an essential key to your sense of self and informs your disposition, identity, and truest nature.

Your moon sign is associated with your internal landscape or your inner emotions. This reflects how you feel about things privately and is linked with your maternal, nurturing side. Your moon sign can show you what hides in your shadows. This is a side people rarely get a glimpse of, and it can show you how you relate to others.

Lastly, your rising sign can be considered the mask you wear when first meeting someone. This reflects how you are perceived by others, and people will interact with this side of you most often. This placement determines all the placements in the houses of your chart, so it is included in your Big Three.

Aries

(MARCH 21 - APRIL 19)

 A new zodiac cycle begins with the sun moving into Aries on the spring equinox. The first house of the zodiac, Aries is a cardinal fire sign, ruled by Mars and named after the god of war. Aries is represented by a charging ram, who storms forward, moving headlong into its next adventure. Aries represents the *I am* presence. These individuals are pioneers who like to go first, which also makes them natural leaders, entrepreneurs, and visionaries. With their fiery and headstrong persona, they are the warriors of the zodiac. The associated birthstones for Aries are aquamarine (March Aries) and diamond (April Aries).

Aries sun signs are courageous leaders. They live at a fast and furious pace that enables them to accomplish many tasks in a short amount of time. The sun in this placement doesn't take no for an answer, which may be viewed as slightly aggressive. Appreciate them for their sense of directness and for always moving the needle forward. The lunar Aries is satisfied only by arousal and spontaneity. Quite the overachiever, they usually get what they want. They may be impulsive or impatient from time to time. The Aries ascendant is ceaselessly enthusiastic, bold, and inspiring, though it may be tough for them to finish their projects once they start them. Sometimes an individual with this placement can feel competitive because they lead with so much passion. Without them, it would be difficult to know what is possible.

Taurus

(APRIL 20 - MAY 20)

 Taurus, the bull, is a fixed earth sign and opens the second house of the zodiac. The bull is ruled by Venus, the planet of love. This means they are all about beauty, sensuality, and giving and receiving love. Taureans are naturally rooted individuals who enjoy consistency, stability, and security. Patient and hardworking, they appreciate the effort it takes to do a job well, though they can sometimes be guilty of procrastination when they are feeling lazy. These types tend to resist change, so they avoid it at all costs. True to their stubborn nature, once they have an idea in their head, it can be rather hard to convince them out of it. The associated birthstones for Taurus are diamond (April Taurus) and emerald (May Taurus).

In its sun placement, the bull is a straight shooter and often plows headfirst into opportunities, seeing them to completion. These individuals are builders by design. Friends may know them to be obstinate, while others view their dedication and perseverance as endearing. Taurus lunar placements are earth mothers and fathers. They feel deeply grounded and connected to the physical world, as well as to their own bodies, desires, and needs. Highly valuing self-care, they nurture their own inner beauty to no end. This moon placement is considered exalted, in a prime placement. They are extremely sensual and appreciate soothing smells, tastes, and touch. Taurus rising placements are practical and loyal. They make devoted partners or best friends if you don't get pushy or try to rush them into things.

Gemini

(MAY 21 - JUNE 20)

Gemini, the celestial twins, sit in the third house of the zodiac. This mutable air placement is ruled by the god and planet Mercury. A sparkly socialite by nature, Gemini thrives in social situations in which they can feel fully expressed. Versatile and ingenious, Geminis always have an excess of mental energy, enough to go around. Though they are curious as a cat, they can be slightly scatterbrained because of the amount of information they are processing all the time. Handle your Gemini with care, as this sign has two sides, and you never know which one you'll be dealing with. This is a perfect representation of polarity within the zodiac. The associated birthstones for Gemini are emerald (May Gemini) and pearl (June Gemini).

Gemini sun placements reveal how to be flexible and adaptable. Whatever the situation, they will be sure to serve up some serious high-spirited energy. A true master of disguise, Gemini sun is a wild card, and this unpredictable placement can embody several personas at any given time. Gemini moon represents a unique genius who glows at the exchange of ideas. This lunar placement needs a constant stream of mental stimulation; otherwise they are easily bored and ready to move on to the next thing. Gemini rising signs are enthralled by the world around them. Floating from here to there, concrete obligations feel like a suffocating trap to this free and relatively unattached sign.

Cancer

(JUNE 21 - JULY 22)

Cancer the crab appears as a hard shell on the outside, while deceptively soft on the inside. This cardinal water sign sits in the fourth house of the zodiac, ruled by the moon. This sign is a homebody at heart, just as a crab carries its home everywhere it roams. Cancers are naturally guarded creatures, fiercely protective of their family and personal affairs. Emotional, sensitive, and intuitive, these individuals feel their way through life and teach how to nurture and honor. They are a reminder that a bit of tenderness can be enough to weather any storm. The corresponding birthstones for Cancer are pearl (June Cancer) and ruby (July Cancer).

The crab in its sun sign expression is highly sensitive, craving personal sanctuary as a reprieve from the physical and emotional world. This sign is in a dance with life, zigzagging between the deep waters of intuition and the safety of grounded shores. The crab sun in its evolved expression is gentle, imaginative, and nurturing. The crab as a lunar placement denotes extra sensitivity to stress and outside factors. They can be moody, demanding, and impractical, requiring more reassurance than most. Being able to establish boundaries is an important life skill for Cancer moons. Cancer in its ascendant sign shows strength, vulnerability, and intimacy. Caregivers by nature, they can teach others about acceptance and tenderness and help those around them break free from their shy hermit shell.

Leo

(JULY 23 – AUGUST 22)

 With a dramatic flourish, Leo the lion roars in the fifth house of the zodiac with an impressive presence. Ruled by the sun, this fixed fire sign prides itself on being able to make practical decisions under fire, for the benefit of many. Known to take charge, they teach others how to surrender to what the moment commands. Ruling compassionately with a generous and big-hearted nature, lions are protective of their pack. Leos demand respect, and often have a way of letting you know. They don't mind being the center of attention; in fact, they expect it. Teaching those around them that it's okay to be seen and heard, Leos are the fiercely loving leaders in the zodiac. The birthstones associated with Leo are ruby (July Leo) and peridot (August Leo).

Leo suns are confident and in charge, usually directing others for a worthy cause. These individuals are pragmatic and organized, and people naturally trust them. They are generally playful, passionate, positive, and supportive. Lunar Leos, on the other hand, can be quite sensitive souls, despite being the king/queen of the land. This sign placement isn't fragile by any means, but they may act wounded if you bruise their delicate ego. Lunar Leos appreciate your understanding of their fiery yet loving nature. Leo ascending is self-assured, charismatic, and proud. If they are not mindful with their words and actions, this confidence can come across as pushy and overbearing. Adored and loved by many, they have an easy time making and keeping friends for a lifetime.

Virgo

(AUGUST 23 – SEPTEMBER 22)

 Virgo, a mutable earth sign, gives guidance into the sixth house of the zodiac. Represented by the Virgin, or goddess of wheat and agriculture, Virgo is ruled by the speedy planet Mercury. Earth-loving Virgo, your presence alone is helpful to others as you are full of actionable answers. These individuals are the realists of the zodiac, as they tend to be orderly, conservative, and analytical. They can grasp a wide view of any situation and use their perspective for the benefit of all involved. Detail oriented and fastidious, they master bringing order to chaos, though they'll often worry their way through it as they go along. This sign possesses a graceful demeanor and highly sensitive nervous system, but they can also be overly critical and project their worries onto others if they aren't mindful. The corresponding birthstones for Virgo are peridot (August Virgo) and sapphire (September Virgo).

Virgo sun is grounded, structured, and reasonable. To make changes, this sign needs to review lots of evidence and prefers the status quo. Lovers of beauty and nature, Virgo suns are devoted, heart-centered, and caring. Lunar Virgo exemplifies perfectionism. This sign could benefit from getting out of its own way, coloring outside the lines, and playing with more magical thinking. Virgo ascending is excellent at both planning and executing practical matters. However, their extreme attention to the particulars can earn them the title of nitpicker if they aren't careful.

Libra

(SEPTEMBER 23 – OCTOBER 22)

 Represented by the scales of justice, the cardinal air sign Libra signifies balance and equanimity. Libra sits in the seventh house of the zodiac and serves as the halfway point in the astrological cycle. Libras are lovers of beauty and it's no wonder, as Venus the planet of love rules this sign. They have a deep yearning to find common ground with others and are typically surrounded by a group of friends. Charismatic and agreeable, Libras possess a magnetic charm. Diplomats of the zodiac, Libras fight for what's right, approaching problems objectively. These individuals care about how others view them, sometimes putting up with more than they would prefer to, to keep the peace. The associated birthstones of Libra are sapphire (September Libra) and opal (October Libra).

The Libra sun has a flair for harmony, fashion, art, style, and all things beautiful. Often thinking in terms of the collective, it's in their highest interest to work toward building a world that supports all ways of life. They model how to appreciate the human vessel and lavishly love their self-care rituals. Lunar Libras love the luxe life and beautification of every kind. These graceful artists are subtle, easygoing charmers who can occasionally languish in their own procrastinations and fantasies. Libra ascendants are known to be optimistic and good-natured, as this sign is often the friend to go to for understanding and advice. They are wonderful teachers of how to consider and listen, but don't expect them to take a side.

Scorpio

(OCTOBER 23 – NOVEMBER 21)

 Scorpio, situated in the eighth house, is ruled over by Pluto, the planet of death and regeneration, which gives this sign its transformative qualities. This fixed water sign is represented by the scorpion. With its piercing pincer, scorpions are poised to strike should a threat come their way. Unfortunately, this also means they occasionally backfire and stab themselves unintentionally. These individuals are intense, and this water element can often feel more like fire. The mysterious Scorpio doesn't mind, as this lends to its power. Leave it to Scorpio to charm their way into your inner realms with a penetrative gaze and enticing gleam in their eye. The associated birthstones for Scorpio are opal (October Scorpio) and topaz (November Scorpio).

Don't let Scorpio sun intimidate you; this dominant placement feels their way through many moods with a brooding and deeply intense demeanor. They don't mean to be off-putting, but they just don't waste time with small talk. Beware your missteps, as this sign deliberately scrutinizes everything with unyielding ferocity. Scorpio moon is comfortable pushing past all limits. This sign can come off as somewhat secretive, but privacy is paramount for them while they obsess over the endless enigmas of the universe. Scorpio ascendant rises out of the ashes like a phoenix reborn. No stranger to the underworld shadows, they recognize that all things must dissolve to be resurrected. This sign is seriously committed to their cause and will stop at nothing to ensure they reach their goals.

Sagittarius

(NOVEMBER 22 – DECEMBER 21)

Sagittarius, ruled by the expansive planet of Jupiter, presides over the ninth house of the zodiac. This mutable fire sign is optimistic, fun, and freedom loving. Sagittarius is represented by the centaur archer, a half-human, half-horse mythological creature, traditionally depicted holding a bow and shooting an arrow. Sagittarians believe the sky is the limit, and this courageous dreamer is here to prove if you can think it, you can do it. This sign is associated with higher learning, and they can often be found with their nose in a book. Known as the travelers of the zodiac, they are great teachers of how to invite in new experiences by adventuring to new places. The associated birthstones for Sagittarius are topaz (November Sagittarius) and tanzanite (December Sagittarius).

An enthusiastic explorer, the Sagittarius sun is always on the move. They tend to come and go without much explanation, which can come off to others as impulsive and erratic (but so much fun it's hard to stay mad at them). Lunar Sagittarius is independent and charismatic, making them a popular crowd-pleaser. Though they are versatile and adaptive in most situations, this sign feels best with their freedom in hand, as they don't like to be tied down.

Sagittarius rising, with their carefree attitude, inspires others to take life lightly. They teach others to expand their horizons. On occasion, their loquacious tongue can get them into hot water, but generally, their good humor can save the day.

Capricorn

(DECEMBER 22 – JANUARY 19)

A mythological sea-goat creature, with the body of a goat and tail of a fish, Capricorn rules over the tenth house of the zodiac. Ruled by Saturn, this cardinal earth sign has a pragmatic and serious demeanor, which makes them highly reliable individuals. Determined and methodical Capricorns are never without a plan, working diligently with focused discipline. This sign is the boss of the zodiac and has a commanding, and rather unheeding, nature. They teach others that slow, deliberate steps and follow-through help maintain and build inner (and outer) resources. The associated birthstones for Capricorn are tanzanite (December Capricorn) and garnet (January Capricorn).

Capricorn sun signs are dependable, stable, and efficient, with a relentless drive to succeed and achieve. They don't mind putting in sincere effort to create a solid foundation in work and life, however, they can come across as stubborn and overbearing if they aren't mindful. Lunar Capricorns have a tough time expressing their emotions and opening up to others. Not wanting to come across as vulnerable, their biggest challenge is identifying and then sharing their feelings with others. Capricorn rising finds unending fulfillment in accomplishing set goals, and they can see all the steps along the way that are needed to lay the foundation and then reach their target. However, they can be highly judgmental if they find you doing something "the wrong way."

Aquarius

(JANUARY 20 – FEBRUARY 18)

 Ruling the new age (the Aquarian Age), Aquarius sits at the eleventh house of the zodiac. Ruled by progressive Uranus, Aquarius is symbolized by the water bearer, and though this sign is connected to (and often associated with) water, it is an expansive air sign. Aquarians are always thinking about the future. These are the humanitarians of the zodiac. They are highly collaborative and community focused. Unafraid to shake things up, this sign is ungovernable and rebellious and the most likely sign to start a grass-roots revolution. This sign is concerned with bringing the human collective together as revered ambassadors of change. The associated birthstones for Aquarius are garnet (January Aquarius) and amethyst (February Aquarius).

Quirky and unique, an Aquarian sun is an innovator, creator, and lover of the strange and unusual. Artists at heart, they are always creating a masterpiece through their love of all things eclectic. This placement can sometimes seem unreliable to friends due to their restless, airy nature. Lunar Aquarians can come off somewhat detached from reality and can even be difficult to understand and interact with. Their sharp mind and quick words redeem them for those willing to overlook their cold demeanor. Aquarius rising signs shine bright as they live to entertain. This sign can see possibilities and potentials where others can't, and they tend to be very understanding and accepting. What you see in yourself as a fault, Aquarius views as your strength. They can be quite unruly at times, and they are almost always up for a challenge.

Pisces

(FEBRUARY 19 – MARCH 20)

 Closing out the zodiac in the twelfth house is Pisces, the fish, a mutable water sign. Pisces is ruled by the dreamy, imaginative planet Neptune. Pisces represents a full cycle through the zodiac, demonstrating mastery on many levels. These sensitive souls are supremely intuitive and display a level of unparalleled psychic prowess. The healers of the zodiac, their level of spirituality feels shamanic and deep. Be careful with your Pisces's feelings, as they are known for their extremely delicate nervous systems and can be particularly vulnerable to rebuffs or rejection. Pisceans teach that all are reflections of one another, and that it's okay to loosen your grip on physical reality occasionally. The associated birthstone for Pisces is amethyst (February Pisces) and aquamarine (March Pisces).

In its sun aspect, Pisces is compassionate and empathetic. This selfless soul knows how to hold your heart gently and with integrity. These individuals are devoted and will always show up for you even in the toughest of times. The lunar Pisces can often be accused of being overly sensitive. Be mindful with your words and actions around them so you don't wound their tender ego. This sign can recharge and rebalance when they get enough alone time. Pisces rising flows with fluidity, and this deep water sign tends to turn on the charm, as they can be people pleasers. When it comes to personal relationships, they must make extra effort to establish boundaries so as not to become someone else's doormat.

OPHIUCHUS, THE THIRTEENTH SIGN

In the days of the ancient Greeks, spring was celebrated on the equinox, beginning in the constellation Aries, with every other sign following in the annual circuit, ending in Pisces. Since then, the procession of Earth's axis has shifted such that the chronology is ever-so-slightly different than it was millennia ago. This phenomenon yields some very interesting results, essentially shifting the constellations one sign over to the west.

Though it is not recognized as an official astrological sign in tropical astrology, Ophiuchus is the sign dominant in the sky for people born between November 29 and December 17. It is represented by the serpent bearer and is known as the forgotten constellation. So what does this mean for all the other signs? Essentially, if Ophiuchus was included in the modern-day grouping, all signs would be slightly off, pushing your sign out by a few days on either end. According to the thirteen zodiac signs, for those of you on the cusp of a sign or born in Sagittarius and surrounding signs, your sun sign would change.

Since astrologers now perform their calculations based on where the planets and sun are relative to the twelve signs (which are fixed), this maintains the traditional twelve signs and reflects the current forecasting methods used today.

Key Takeaways

This chapter was packed with information to guide you on your exploration of the twelve astrological signs. Let's recap some of the highlights you'll want to remember as you move on to exploring the planets and cosmic luminaries.

◆ The way you react, respond, think, feel, and behave can all be mapped through the signs.

◆ There are twelve zodiac signs in modern astrology. The astrological year begins at the spring equinox with Aries and moves along to Pisces, which closes the astrological year.

- Degrees within a chart bring more meaning to each placement. They denote qualities and characteristics of the signs.

- Each sign comprises 30 degrees, with each sign ranging from 0 to 29 degrees. The entire astrological wheel represents the full 360 degrees of the zodiac.

- The signs each have a ruling planet or luminary body, element, modality, birthstone, and other variables that create a unique zodiac profile.

- Take time to get familiar with the hallmarks of each sign so that you can better recognize them when they appear in your readings.

CHAPTER FIVE

The Planets

he zodiac signs illuminate how the planets work within you, and the planets represent facets of yourself, including your mind, emotions, the way you love and your drive, to name a few. This chapter will focus on the planets and luminary bodies that are represented through astrology. You'll notice quickly that Earth isn't included in the zodiac as a planet. Though it seems strange to leave out the planet on which we live, this is because astrology is a measurement of the planets in relation to Earth. Therefore, Earth is considered the constant in the astrological equation.

While the planets play the parts of you that interact with the signs, the signs show how they are represented in you. They can be reserved or outgoing, enthusiastic or mellow. The signs and planets dance together to create a beautiful symphony. Once the "where" of the houses is added, you can start to build a bigger picture of the areas of life that are affected and begin to use the planets to create stories that help build your holistic astrological portrait.

What Are the Planets?

These celestial powerhouses hold great influence over your chart and are an essential piece of the zodiac puzzle. When interpreting charts, there are many subtle and explicit power dynamics that play out between the planets, signs, houses, and aspects. The planets must function under the sign style that they reside in, and each sign has a ruling planet. The ruling planet simply means that the planet has an affinity for the sign, and that they play well together. For example, Jupiter rules the sign Sagittarius, which represents luck. Other signs may also feel lucky when they are going through a Jupiter transit or house. The ruling planets are the bosses in the zodiac and determine how the signs will behave in their presence.

Since there are only nine planets, and Earth is not included in this portion of the astrowheel, some planets rule more than one sign. For example, Mercury and Venus each rule two signs. The sun and moon are included in the groupings because although they are not planets, these luminary bodies hold great influence over life on Earth. The planets are grouped into personal (inner) and outer (collective) planets, depending on where they are situated in their orbits around the sun. The planets are traditionally categorized as feminine (yin) and masculine (yang), though a modernized view of this classification might prefer to label these as night and day or nocturnal (of the night) and diurnal (of the day). Though the masculine and feminine show up in historical archetypes, it feels limiting to simplify the qualities of these otherworldly astral bodies to a binary gender.

The Sun

 Radiating with light and warmth, the sun is the luminary body that represents your conscious mind, personal power, and outward-facing ego. Ruling fiery Leo and the fifth house, this is the central star around which all else is organized in the solar system. The word *solar* means "sun," and all other planets revolve around it. Many ancient cultures have holidays celebrating the sun because this celestial light brings life to many. In a chart, this means the creation of life purpose and derived meaning, under the guidance of this significant star. It shines brightly for all to see and helps define your core personality. The sun is who you are in your heart and what fulfills your purpose. It is associated closely with your vitality and essential energies of how you show up in the world.

Sunday is the day of the week associated with the sun, and it should come as no surprise that the sun possesses diurnal (of the day) properties, which have traditionally been considered masculine. The yang vibrations the sun gives off are energizing, activating, and invigorating. The power color of the sun is yellow or gold, which invokes joy, exuberance, and optimism. The sun represents the "here and now" and the lens under which you'll develop much of your personal psychological bias. Though you may hope and dream to be many things, the sun is simply what you are. To act out your sun sign is to act with purpose, directing your creativity and passions in an aligned way.

The Moon

 Signaling the emergence of night and the end of day, the moon is a deep self-reflective well. It is the luminary body that holds your subconscious and represents your emotional nature. In astrology, this is the side of you that is associated with your inner world and internal thoughts. This is the side that people don't see because it represents a world of feelings. The dark side of the moon is your shadowy subconscious, and this can be thought of as the "unknown-unknown," or your subconscious blind spots. This lunar celestial satellite rules over watery Cancer and the fourth house of the zodiac. Like the intuitive crab, lunar energy is deep, personal, receptive, and instinctual. The moon embodies all your private, unexpressed thoughts as it reflects who you are on the inside as well as your securities.

As the sun gives off light, the moon receives light and thus its primary energy is nocturnal or yin. It's traditionally associated with feminine energy, as it is both inner child and inner mother. The ebb and flow of the moon rules rhythms as well as natural earth and body cycles. The moon is associated with "moon-day" (*lundi* in French), or Monday, and the color white, as it reflects all the colors in the prismatic light spectrum. The color white represents purity, innocence, and simplicity. To act out your moon energies is acting upon your instinctual and automatic emotional responses out of spontaneity rather than by design.

Mercury

Mercury is both the smallest and the fastest-revolving planet in the solar system and comes up next in the planetary tour as the first planet in the solar system. It rules the signs of Gemini and Virgo and therefore also rules the third and sixth houses of communication and details/daily routine, respectively. Hermes, the messenger of the gods in Greek mythology, is associated with Mercury, who governs the transfer of ideas and communication in all forms. This planet rules the signs of Gemini and Virgo, cruising the intellectual superhighway at breakneck speeds. It represents the mind, intelligence, and perception. A placement here indicates the style in which your inner philosopher responds to earthly experiences. In other words, both houses in which Mercury rules have strong effects on your personal growth as it relates to your environment.

Mercury is associated with Wednesday (*mercredi* in French) and the colors brown or green. Brown signifies earth or soil, while green represents nature, renewal, and fertility. Traditionally, Mercury is neither day nor night energies, neither masculine nor feminine. Mercury is considered a neutral nonbinary blend of energies (as is Uranus). This gives it qualities of both genders. To act out your Mercurial energies is to use your perception to access your technical abilities and communicative expression. Depending on the placement of Mercury in your chart, it can show up as wit, fastidiousness, nervous or high-strung energy, or obsessive-compulsive thoughts or behavior.

Venus

Venus has a quick 243-day rotation cycle around the sun. As the second planet from the sun, it's the planet closest to Earth. Venus is the champion of love, romance, and all creature comforts. It's traditionally associated with the goddess of love, though its complicated gender association may surprise you. Mercury isn't the only ruler of multiple signs. Venus rules over both Taurus and Libra. These signs are connected to self-care, beauty, and sensuality. The essence of this planetary rule is all about how you celebrate yourself and derive pleasure from life. As a symbol of all that is seen, touched, tasted, smelled, heard, and felt, Venusian energy rules the senses. It values the arts, harmony, and meditation, and, on the flip side, inertia, and indecisiveness.

The day of the week associated with Venus is Friday (*vendredi* in French) and the colors green and pink. These are both heart chakra colors and represent earth and air elements contained within. Green is indicative of abundance and fertility, and pink stands for harmony, affection, and Universal love. Though Venus has earned a reputation for being a feminine planet in modern astrology because it governs both diurnal (yang) and nocturnal (yin) signs, this planet is nonbinary. Because of its blend of energies, this planet can feel neutral, as it's associated with both the morning star and evening star. Venus in your chart can reflect your sentiments, values, pleasures, artistic tastes, and what makes you happy.

Mars

 The third planet from the sun, Mars, slowly laps the sun every 687 days. Governing fiery Aries and the eighth house, Mars earns its name from the god of war. Mars energy is described as ambitious, strident, and somewhat competitive. This planetary energy ignites through passion, purpose, and planning. This energy embodies leadership, desire, courage, motivation, and sex drive. On the other hand, it is also associated with aggression, impatience, impulsiveness, and anger. Whichever way you look at it, Mars is the planet of action, rather than reaction. Depending on where Mars is in your chart, you can begin to tell how your temperament is expressed, what makes you angry, and what your instinctual response will be toward those inputs. The position of Mars by house indicates the areas of life in which you express the most enthusiasm, assertion, and self-actualization.

Tuesday (*mardi* in French) is the day of the week associated with Mars. Martian energy is also symbolized by the color red. Red is a particularly intense color and can span the spectrum of emotional associations (love/hate, passion/anger, determination/danger). When you see this color, you may experience strong emotions, which is par for the course for Mars. Martian energy is a diurnal (yang) energy because it seeks to accomplish, lead, and direct. When acting out your Mars tendencies, you are direct, self-assured, and adventurous.

ASTEROIDS AND COMETS

Although not planets or luminary bodies, the presence of asteroids and comets plays a role in your chart. Physically, the two are very similar, with their main differences being composition (asteroids are rocky, metal material, while comets are mostly ice and dust). Both possess orbital patterns, and so both can be worked into an astrological reading.

When either of these appear in a transit or personal planetary alignment, you might want to include them while you examine your chart, as this is when their largest expression manifests. For example, the presence of a comet in the sky usually signals great change, as historically these have ushered in both human and natural disasters. The presence of asteroids, however, have a gentler connotation, as they are traditionally considered feminine (yin) energy.

Each asteroid is typically named after a goddess in either the Greek or Roman pantheon: Pallas, Juno, Vesta, and Ceres. They are each associated with a quality of that goddess and represent humanity's modern consciousness embracing the dimensions and shades of sacred femininity. Comets such as Halley's, Hale-Bopp, and Hyakutake bring revolutionary, innovative, and dramatic energy.

Jupiter

Jupiter, revolving around the sun every twelve years, rules the sign Sagittarius and the ninth and twelfth houses. Situated farther away from the sun, Jupiter represents the first of the outer planets, which can be considered the transpersonal or collective planets. The equivalent of the Greek god Zeus, the Roman god Jupiter roughly translates in Latin to "sky father." An archetype of expansion, abundance, and success, this is the planet of opportunity in all forms. Jupiter's placement in your chart points to areas in your life that are advantageously opportunistic. Eternally optimistic, this planet in your chart is auspicious and signals growth, so it is generally viewed as positive wherever it shows up.

Thursday (*jeudi* in French) is the day of the week ruled by Jupiter. Jupiter energy is symbolized by orange. Orange blends the intensity and passion of red with the cheerful optimism of yellow. Since Jupiter rules over fiery Sagittarius, it is considered masculine/yang energy. This is the energy of accomplishment, achieving, learning, growing, and amplification. When you are working with Jupiter energies within your chart, they symbolize freedom, generosity, and luck, as well as the teacher or guru energy. Consider Jupiter to be the prophet of evolution. On the other hand, it may indicate overextension and overdoing it, so be mindful to note where Jupiter appears within your houses.

Saturn

 Saturn rules Capricorn and the tenth house with orderly precision. This planet, thought to be cosmic law enforcement, is the last you can see with your naked eye, as it is the second of the outer planets and very far away from the sun. Representing outside authority, boundaries, rules, maturity, and elderhood, Saturn takes twenty-nine years to revolve around the sun. This orbital cycle is commonly known as your Saturn return. It represents a time of contraction and shadow work, which emerge for you to take a closer look at the blind spots in your life. Because of its long rotation cycle, this planet comes around only a few times per lifetime, and when it does, it signals complete reorganization of foundational systems, the onset of challenges, and lessons that point to understanding your edges.

Saturday, or "Saturn-day," is the day of the week that Saturn rules. Saturn is symbolized by the neutral color gray. This color evokes a conservative, formal, and sophisticated vibration and is relatively calm and devoid of emotion. As a rather diplomatic color, it represents timeless balance in astrology. Saturn is here to balance out big and bold Jupiter. Because of this balancing effect, Saturnian energies bring sensible awareness and responsibility to keep all energies in check. These energies are also considered to symbolize time as a process, including aging, decay, and death. Saturn is traditionally considered diurnal (yang) energy in a chart because of its discipline and stewardship.

Uranus

Uranus, ruling Aquarius and the eleventh house, completes its circle around the sun every eighty-four years. As the seventh planet from the sun, Uranus is an outer planet, with a long orbital track. Its energy is considered collective, applying to many. This means that it brings its rebellious, revolutionary tones about once a lifetime. Uranus feels radical, progressive, and intellectual in nature. Placements here involve big societal shifts and technological advancements. It is not a personally influential planet, though if a personal planet aligns with Uranus or it conjuncts at an angle in your chart, its interpretation would be more relevant for you. When it shows up like this in your chart, it can indicate innovation, personal changes, initiative, and personal freedom. Think of Uranus as the unconventional genius who uses their unique gifts for the betterment, modernization, and advancement of humanity.

Uranus wasn't commonly included in the Greek calendar because it went unnoticed until the telescope was engineered much later in history. Therefore, Uranus, along with Neptune and Pluto, are not associated with days of the week. Uranus is symbolized by the color pale blue, which is linked to the throat chakra, or themes of expression and intuition. Uranian presence suggests an "awakening" factor is at play, as aspects and transits bring upheaval, shocks, and sudden changes. These are necessary forces that move through the collective to bring about evolution and consciousness upgrades.

Neptune

Neptune, ruling watery Pisces and the twelfth house of the zodiac, cycles round the sun once every 165 years and is named after the god of the sea. Neptune is a superdense planet, which is over 80 percent covered by water and ice. Because it moves slowly and spends over fourteen years in a sign, it's also (along with Pluto) considered to be a generational influencer. This outer planet typically ushers in evolutionary change as part of the collective experience. As the planet of dreams and spirituality, placement here evokes imagination, transcendence, and dissolving of boundaries and realities. When Neptune shows up in your chart aligned with a personal planet or transit, expect radical shift. Personal ideals could come up to be examined, as well as an opening or expansion of your natural intuitive gifts.

Neptune symbolizes spirituality and compassion, yet it is also the domain of dreams and illusions. Because of this, Neptune placements can activate your psychic senses and amp your dream-state experiences. Use care and be aware with these placements, as they can also signal confusion and delusion showing up in certain areas of your chart. The color indigo or purple represent Neptune, as this is a color denoting psychic properties, wisdom, and spirituality. This planet is a mysterious one, but its energy brings inspiration if you are open to receiving it. Traditionally this is thought of as nocturnal or yin energy, holding both the energy of chaos and creativity simultaneously.

Pluto

Pluto, ruling watery Scorpio and the eighth house of the zodiac, is the planet farthest from the sun. With its 248-year cycle, Pluto is a dwarf planet whose name comes from the god of the underworld. Its slow rotation and elliptical orbit means that it can stay in a sign for anywhere from nine to thirty years. Plutonian energy is a deep internal well of the soul. It is the shamanic shadow work ushering in intense transformation. Because Pluto is on the fringe of the solar system, these shifts mostly affect the collective experience, though it can also be felt in a tangible way when it aligns or transits personal planets or angles. Harnessing the power of the light to cut through your darkest challenges and fears, Pluto exemplifies total transformation. This energy can feel empowering but can also appear in a chart when you feel powerless and karmically wounded.

Plutonian placements can signal psychological depth, desire to evolve, and all things considered taboo (sex, depression, obsessions). Pluto is symbolized by the color black. As the ruler of Scorpio, the death theme is present. It seems natural then that Pluto is seen as a nocturnal (yin) planet. This planet is best approached with caution and a mentality of sweet surrender. The more you can relinquish your need to control, the easier the transition through these transits will feel. Keep your psyche healthy with the understanding that all things must destruct or die out before they can come back together again stronger, and every beginning also has an end.

UNDERSTANDING CHIRON

Chiron, the wounded healer, represents another archetype in astrology. Named after the Greek centaur (half horse, half man), Chiron was immortal and carried a painful wound that would not heal. Eventually, Chiron was set free from his immortality so that he could embrace death and release himself from eternal suffering. Chiron symbolizes a point in one's chart where one has succeeded and overcome great loss (wounding) and has transmuted that pain into valuable lessons. Chiron energy helps create healing because it's been through the process before and can now lead by example.

Chiron was first discovered in 1977 as an asteroid but underwent a small identity upgrade so that it's now classified as a minor planet. Orbiting between strict Saturn and revolutionary Uranus, Chiron is considered a mystical mediator. When you see Chiron popping up in your chart, this represents past life lessons that have come full circle and your ability to hold wounding in order to uniquely serve another's healing journey. Its presence reminds you that to live is to survive your wounds. It is a reminder that you have a tremendous capacity for growth through your own healing and that you can help others going through similar circumstances.

Retrograde Planets

All planets have retrogrades except for the sun and the moon. During retrograde periods, planets seem to move backward in their orbits. This is an illusion, yet retrogrades seem to have a profound effect on collective transits. For example, you probably have heard of Mercury retrograde (Rx). Mercury retrograde is a period when the planet Mercury appears to spin backward or "retreat" in the sky. During this time, it is a common belief that communication, technology, and relationships are affected (sometimes negatively). To have the best chance at "surviving" Mercury Rx, it's suggested to drop into stillness. That means no signing contracts, no making or carrying out important decisions, and no forward momentum.

The phenomenon seems to affect people worldwide, though there are a few who experience enhanced effects when retrogrades come around. For example, if you have a positive Mercury placement in your chart, you may be relatively unaffected or even blessed through a retrograde. During retrogrades for all planets, it is common to see a "return" or repeat of cycles, as people and experiences appear to come back into your life. For example, this is a time when exes may attempt to reenter your life. Though it's perfectly acceptable and advised to revisit certain goals and deadlines you've set for yourself during these times, in general, retrogrades can be seen as a more temporary visitation. Anything that attempts to cycle back in will have to stand the test of time by making it through the retrograde portal to the other side in order for it to hold staying power.

Key Takeaways

You've learned so much in this chapter, and there is always more to learn. Let's quickly recap the main points to help keep things organized as you move into exploring the houses of the zodiac.

◆ There are eight planets and two luminary bodies represented in modern astrology. Omitting Earth, and including the sun and the moon, these make up the inner and outer planets.

◆ The inner planets are known as personal planets, while the outer planets are known as transcendent planets, which affect the collective.

◆ Each planet rules over a sign (and Mercury and Venus each govern two). Rulership means this planet gives insight into the core traits and personality of the sign it's in.

◆ Asteroids and comets can influence your birth chart, so keep an eye out for their transits.

◆ Planets can appear as retrograde, or moving backward in the sky. During this time, pay attention to things breaking down and take time to rest and reflect in stillness instead of pushing to get things done.

CHAPTER SIX

The Twelve Houses

ow that you have learned about the signs and the planets, it's time to take a plunge into the houses of the zodiac. Because a horoscope, or astrological chart, comprises many complex elements, these elements must have a way to be integrated so they can be summarized and made into a cohesive story. Remember that the planets and luminary bodies represent the "what" in your cosmic blueprint, and the signs demonstrate how these play out in your life. The houses, then, symbolize where these stories take place. These are the areas of life or fields of expertise in which the drama of the planets and signs collide.

There are twelve houses and many different systems used to divide the horoscope. The system you'll be learning is the called the Placidus system. Though there are multiple house systems, there is general agreement that the horizon or ascendant begin in the first house of Aries, and the midheaven starts in the tenth house. Houses are important because someone with a sun in Gemini in the third house will have a totally different life experience from someone with a Gemini sun in the tenth house. By bringing dimension to the areas of your birth chart, houses really begin to pull together a fuller picture of who you are.

What Are the Twelve Houses?

The twelve houses are the segments created when the zodiac wheel (360 degrees) is split into equal pieces. Each house represents thirty degrees of the zodiac and is governed by a sign with a ruling planet. They act as homes for the planets in your chart. The horoscope is further divided into two hemispheres and four quadrants. Each hemisphere has six houses, and each quadrant has three houses. In general, the bottom half (first through sixth houses) of a zodiac chart represent the personal life, while the top hemisphere moves into more group, shared, and collective ideals.

There are ways of interpreting charts that place focus on the "empty" areas of your horoscope. Mainly, this can be thought of as areas where you seek or deny expression. Think about these spaces in a chart as the areas in which you've already achieved mastery and no longer need to focus. Despite there being many ways of interpreting a chart, for now let's keep things simple and reference only the houses with symbols (planets), transits, or activity in them.

The twelve houses symbolize the areas of primary focus where most of your dramas will unfold. Each house has a nature that is either conducive or counter-productive to certain pursuits, as we will explore in the coming chapter. When studying the houses, you can bring the planets a little closer to home, grounding the celestial orchestra into an earthbound symphony. Let's look at them individually to catch a closer glimpse of what they are.

First House: I Am

Traditionally known as the house of the self, this is the "me, myself, and I" place that is considered the most important house of the zodiac. Representing life and breadth, this is the house of birth through the early years of life. This house is ruled by Aries/Mars and inside it, you'll find invaluable insight into your own health and vitality, as well as how you are perceived by others. Think of it as the home of first impressions. The first house also symbolizes your appearance, self-image, and your physical body, which is closely linked to the sign Aries, which governs this house. This house deals with perception, your mannerisms, way of being, and how you see yourself before you begin to mature and evolve. It represents your birth experience and sponta-neous gut reactions to outside stimuli.

The first house holds the ascendant, which is the house of the rising sun. *Horoskopos*, meaning "hour marker," is another word for the ascendant. Spiritually, this is the moment a new soul begins its journey into the world. This diurnal (yang) house traditionally helps you guide and navigate through the world. Planets in this house are particularly amplified. For example, Taurus in the first house individuals may be particularly stubborn, and Aquarians in the first house may be detached from reality by an otherworldly degree. This house, like all things, is neither good nor bad, but planets here are emphatically pronounced and expressed. For example, someone with Mars in the first house will find it natural to assert themselves, take a leadership role, or become health conscious.

Second House: I Have

The house of resources, the second house, is ruled by Taurus/Venus. This is the realm of matter, self-sufficiency, and sensuality. This house is closely linked to your possessions, especially money, work, values, habits, and priorities. Even your work ethic can be found here, which is your dedication to putting in effort to receive reward. All things seen, touched, tasted, smelled, and heard are included here, and its primary energy is nocturnal (yin). What is it that you value? Your home, your belongings, and all the items you hold most dear are cherished here.

Your ability to handle your personal resources are affected by the planets and signs in this house. Transits in this sign often challenge your relationship to money or your understanding between the material and nonmaterial world. It can highlight your values. For example, Jupiter in this house would prove to be advantageous because it represents wild financial capacity and opportunity to create prosperity. No matter what you put your mind to, you'll generate abundance for yourself (which can oftentimes be much more than income). It may also indicate an overattachment to your funds or your funds deriving your self-worth (which is never a great measure of true success). In traditional astrology, your talents and self-esteem are also included in the second house.

Third House: I Speak

The third house of the zodiac is ruled by Gemini/Mercury. This is the house of communication and intellect. This house is diurnal (yang) energy, and it's a rather passive house (as opposed to later houses dealing with death and imprisonment). Some houses tend to be more observant in nature, and the third house is no exception. Here, you'll hone your perception and expression abilities as you interact with friends, siblings, family members, neighbors, your local community, and your daily environment. This covers your local commute and places around you that you frequent. This house deals with lower education (formative years), language, contracts, and media. In this sector, you find your voice, develop writing skills, articulation, and evolve your expression.

The third house is favorable to the planet Mercury, its ruler. It is also considered the house of joy for moon placements. This means the moon feels at home here. There are so many associations with the moon in this house, including the link to ancient Egyptian god Thoth (god of scribes), who is associated with Mercury, ruler of the third house. Lastly, the third house deals with your mind and thoughts. When signs or planets come into this house, they affect your exchanges with others, with varying shades of their own "flavor." For example, a third house in Aries might mean your mind moves quickly and that you're an independent thinker. You might be short-tempered or prone to arguing on occasion, as is the Aries nature.

Fourth House: I Nurture

The fourth house of the zodiac is ruled by Cancer and the moon. This house is all about nurturing, family, home, roots, and self-care. The nocturnal/yin nature of the fourth house radiates lovingly to any planets or signs that play within it. This house naturally has a soft and inviting feel, and this is where you can hone your receptivity. Though it may seem easy to receive, this is a gentle practice that takes time to fully embrace. The moon, ruler of the house, speaks to mothering/parenting and children. This is the abode of the "lowest heaven," touching the lowest part of the wheel and informing our foundations. Since this part of the house is closest to earth, it touches matters of the land and everything below it (minerals, oil, mining, etc.).

The roots that this house holds speak to your emotional needs, both conscious and subconscious. By tracing your origins, ancestors, and lineage, you can unearth family patterns and dynamics that influence your daily life. The fourth house also represents the sale or purchase of a new home. The effects of planets and signs here are the most pronounced during childhood. In fact, the first four houses deal mostly with birth to adolescence. Transits and planetary action here primarily describe the shape of home and family life in your formative years. For example, a sun in the fourth house will not be happy unless their home life is/was happy.

Fifth House: I Love

The fifth house is ruled by Leo and the sun. This is the house of creativity, expression, joyful play, relationships, romance, and fertility. Known traditionally as Bona Fortuna, this is the house of good fortune. As a solar/diurnal/yang energy, this is the place where you live out your highest expression. As you step more fully into your authentic joy, you develop creativity. This is the light you shine in the world, and here you find all sorts of expression: art, entertainment, and theatrical. Hobbies, including recreation and sports, are included here in the fifth house. If you're thinking of starting a family, conception, fertility, pregnancy, adoption, and children come up here as well.

Your placements here denote how you like to have fun and enjoy life. The fifth house governs indulgences of all shapes and forms, including holidays, gambling, risk, luxuries, parties, and places of leisure. Risky sex is represented here as well, so here is where you'll find love affairs. This house is about as exotic as it gets, and a loaded fifth house infers "let the good times roll." Anything pleasure related belongs to this house. Too much of a good thing could turn sour, though, so watch out for a loaded fifth house. Placements here enjoy delights and satisfy their senses so placements here are mostly considered advantageous. The sun, its ruler, feels at home here, as well as Venus, which particularly glitters from this spot.

Your natal planets are the planets that are designated and consistent in your birth chart at the moment you were born. Transits are a way of describing planetary movement across a natal chart. If a planet is transiting your chart, it's moving through, and the planetary transits are akin to orbital cycles. For it to be considered a transit, the planet must pass between Earth and the sun. It's important to note that the inner planets have relatively short and therefore quick transits, while the outer planets have longer orbital periods, so their transits takes much longer. To determine whether a transit is positive or detrimental, you'll also want to look at the aspects (which will be covered in a later chapter).

As transits can interpret ongoing movement, they are focused on planetary returns. A return chart is something you can make for any planet, and the benefit here is that it can measure and forecast upcoming cycles in your life. It is popular to use the sun as a planetary return because the solar return is something familiar—365 days and very predictable. Another noteworthy return is the Saturn return, occurring every twenty-nine years at ages twenty-nine, fifty-eight, and eighty-seven. This one can dig up some shadows and be very confronting, but since you can forecast its onset, you can plan ahead for this one.

Sixth House: I Serve

The sixth house, ruled by Virgo/Mercury, is the house of work and health. Known in traditional astrology as the house of Mala Fortuna, or "bad fortune," this house signals a big comedown from the fifth house. This energy is a nocturnal/yin energy meant to balance the fifth house. Since the body and your vitality are represented by the first house (Aries), the health referred to here is more the absences of health, illness, or what you need to focus on (some examples are nutrition, weight loss, exercise, cleaning, and hygiene). The presence of a planetary or sign placement here represents the adverse effects health is having on your life. This house also deals with animals and pets. Of course, it wouldn't be a house of bad fortune if it didn't also deal with accidents, so they're also thrown in with the bunch.

The sixth house highlights a need to be useful in the world, though service here is more concerned with the work it takes to build something, brick by brick, than a career focus (which is found in the tenth house). Expressed here is your daily work experience, errands, housework, chores, your contributions to the world, nature of your work, and lifestyle. Developmentally, this house is a bridge between adolescence and adulthood, as we mature and become concerned with creating order in the world. For Mars, this is the traditional house of joy, and this placement is quite favorable, though any planet here will be showing up to do the hard work needed to succeed.

Seventh House: I Partner

The seventh house is ruled by Libra/Venus in its diurnal/yang energy. This day incarnation is like a breath of fresh air coming from the sixth house, which felt contracted, to a renewal of energy. This is the home of the descendant, or the point opposite the ascendant. This sign is the sign descending in the sky at the exact moment of your birth. This point represents who and what you are attracted to and what you attract to you. This area is ripe for romance. The seventh house energy begins to move away from the personal and into the outer world, starting with interpersonal relationships, and how we get along with others. This house also includes coworkers or business relationships, one-on-one dynamics, important friendships, and adult children.

Another area that comes up in the seventh house is projection of others. As Carl Jung called it, the "disowned self." This can be thought of as a shadow part, which is self-denied, but can be triggering to view within others. Though the deeper meaning it holds is that it is a part of yourself requiring integration, some astrologers think of this concept as an enemy. This house is also where romantic partnership, living together, union, and marriage are seen. Though marriage is included here, this house is more about attraction, meeting someone, and the initial connection. When placements or transits occur here, seek to understand the energy given to others and your need to connect to create lasting bonds.

Eighth House: I Release

In the eighth house, ruled by Scorpio/Pluto, there is a plunge into darkness. With Pluto as a ruler, it's no surprise that this house governs birth, death, and rebirth. If you're seeking the transformation sector of your chart, look no further. Though it is nocturnal/yin energy, this area of a chart can be quite challenging because it represents the dark womb of nothingness. This place must be reached to transcend or to rise above; dissolution is a necessary evil. The eighth house points to mysteries, secrets, deep fears, mental issues, anxieties, and abuse of power. Collective resources, such as debts, loans, taxes, inheritance, and other people's money, also show up here.

Placements in this area of the chart can be intimidating. Think of it as Kali Ma energy, the Hindu goddess who is both the bringer of death and the giver of life. This house forces you to reckon with your relationship to loss. You could look at this as how gently you are able to release. Are you the type who holds on until the ship sinks, or can you cut your losses while you are still ahead? Either way, if you can learn to accept these natural cycles, it bodes well for how you fare on the other side of the rebirth portal. Though no planet or transit fares particularly well here, the "dark night of the soul" process can be very healing and liberating if viewed with the right attitude. This house can and will strengthen a person.

Ninth House: I Explore

The ninth house, ruled by Sagittarius/Jupiter, leads from the darkness and into the light. Whether traveling abroad or journeying inside the heart/mind, this house energizes and brings boundless joy and optimism to your adventures. Traditionally labeled "the house of God," this nickname stems from its ruler, Jupiter, who was the king of gods. It is here you may find yourself asking for the deeper meaning of life, questions such as "Why am I here, and what is my higher purpose?" In the ninth house, you engender personal growth as you stretch your consciousness. Higher pursuits, philosophy, and personal beliefs all reside here. This includes collegiate experiences and graduate school or any higher learning you study. Religion, clergy, and churches live here, as does spirituality. Meditation, gurus, and mysticism all hold a place for the seeker in the ninth house.

This day/yin energy is a complementary place for its ruler as well as the sun (the ninth house is its house of joy). This expansive energy radiates far and wide, permeating and drenching us all with its omnipotence and contagious high-spirited energy. When a planet or sign comes into this house, it's generally viewed as a positive thing, unless it happens to be Saturn, which usually contracts your travels. It is here that you can reflect on wisdom seeking, freedom, truth, and knowledge of the natural world and nature of existence. However you interpret the ninth house energies, think big, as this house pushes you toward fun and exciting new horizons.

Tenth House: I Aspire

The tenth house, ruled by Capricorn/Saturn, is by far the most public part of your horoscope. This house deals with career, contributions, and life's mission. For an evolved soul in this house, both career and passion in life will aspire to be aligned, complementary, or one and the same. This house is all about your public presentation, including your reputation, image, and social status, making it the most visible spot in your chart. Keep in mind that with visibility comes the good and the bad, the admiration and contempt. These dynamics can be so powerful that some astrologers believe this to be the second-most-important house in your chart, second only to the first house. The highest point of your chart, the midheaven (MC), is located at the cusp of this house, representing your raison d'être, or reason for being.

Though this house is a public-facing segment of your personal astrology, the energy it holds is nocturnal/yin, rather than daytime energy. This means that this is a place for reflection and receiving feedback. When planets transit this house, your success, reputation, and career are up for review. Planets with afflicted aspects can deny these things in your chart or seek to undo progress here. Here we see how we hold up in the court of public opinion. This house also represents the role of the father or disciplinarian in your family, judges, authority, the law, and employers. Recognition is highlighted here as well through prestige, fame, distinction, and social standing.

Eleventh House: I Innovate

The eleventh house, ruled by Aquarius/Uranus, is traditionally known as the house of good spirits. This is a community house reflecting both on humanity as a whole and your social connections with others. This house represents social progress, innovation, activism, groupthink, and collective hopes. This space involves a great network of acquaintances, including allies, friends, helpers, friend groups, clubs, and contacts we amass throughout life. The web is far and deep. The eleventh house also represents your relationship to hope and future-focused goals. Stepchildren and other people's children are additionally included in the eleventh house.

This house is a diurnal/yang energy, breathing life into your friendships, and it is generally regarded as positive when placements transit here. Because this house is ruled by an outer sign and planet, it also deals with points that are outside of the self. Included here are matters of government, politics, and people of power. This is quite an idealistic house, and broader concepts also show up here, such as freedom, support, and assistance. Though this is usually a pleasant part of your chart, afflicted planets can fracture friendships, cause chaos, or create a sense of despair or hopelessness. In this house, you detach from imposed rules that the tenth house creates and sustains and go about things in your own way. The eleventh house planets will show you how you embrace your own freedom of creation as well as reveal your unique independence.

Twelfth House: I Dream

The twelfth house, ruled by Pisces/Neptune, is the house of the subconscious. All things that are hidden reside here in the clandestine final house of the zodiac. With a prevalent nocturnal/yin energy, you are alone in the mists in a womb that feels empty yet contains all your deepest secrets. Here you deal with what you are hiding from others. To access the place inside that is needed to bring these matters to light, you may want to try past-life-regressions, hypnosis, or shamanic healing, as this house deals with the nebulous world of what lies beneath. Here you look at lifting the veil to reveal places just beyond your conscious perception.

In modern astrology, the twelfth house includes softer topics, like mysticism, trance, psychic states, and dreams. Since the dream state is a liminal realm, this house governs all spaces in between the *no longer* and *not yet*. It is a gray area between worlds typically associated with transitional times and can be an ending and a beginning. It is a departure into the mysteries of the unknown, yet it can be symbolic of a space to heal and explore the neutral energies of the void. In traditional astrology, seclusion and secluded places are grouped in the twelfth house. This includes prisons, hospitals, monasteries, and private resorts. Transits in this house remind you that not all things are meant to last and that all things have a deeper meaning if you can embrace the subtle energy or intention behind them.

Key Takeaways

This chapter contained a great deal of information pertaining to the houses of the zodiac, looking at their inherent meaning, and what they symbolize. Here is a quick recap of what was covered:

- The house system used in this book is called the Placidus system, though there are a few modern systems astrologers use, so be mindful in your analysis to check which system an astrologer might be referencing.

- Houses provide the "where" aspect to help create the scene where the dramas in your life will act out their scenes.

- Even if two people have the same exact sun sign, they may have different placements within the houses (for example, Leo in the first house and Leo in the fourth house). The life experiences will be totally different.

- The bottom hemisphere of the horoscope chart deals with the self and personal life, while the top half of the chart starts to move into public and collective spaces, community, and idealism.

- Transits involve tracking and interpreting the movement of the planets through an astrological chart. Planets and signs have transits.

Part 3

APPLYING ASTROLOGY TO LIFE

Now that we have studied the signs, the planets, and the houses, you are well equipped to add some depth to your astroknowledge. The upcoming chapters will cover how to apply all the different parts of astrology into a cohesive storyline through chart reading and analysis. This part of the book takes everything you know about your horoscope and begins to synthesize the information into digestible pieces so that your practical application makes sense, not only to you but also to others for whom you are reading.

We'll cover reading your birth chart basics, moon phases, and angles and aspects. I'll be providing some sample birth chart readings so you can have some working samples to model your readings on. This will help add color to a basic reading by giving your readings greater dimension. The following chapters touch on interpreting your chart and then cover the major areas your sun sign affects including your health and self-care, romance and relationships, and work and career. The most exciting part? By the end of this segment, you'll be able to perform a reading for yourself.

CHAPTER SEVEN

Reading and Interpreting Your Birth Chart

his chapter will bring you closer to developing your own individual reading style as your astrological skills mature. You will begin to inspect the various elements that will create a full picture of your horoscope, first by looking more deeply at your natal chart and then by studying signs, planets, and houses. You'll briefly touch on aspects and angles, though the full scope of those components is considered an advanced topic in astrology and won't be a necessary tool for you to begin conducting basic readings.

You will also be introduced to the moon's nodes and phases and how they can impact a chart, reflecting even more clarity and depth as you decipher the inherent meaning. Included in this section are some sample birth charts so you can see examples of how you might hypothetically apply your newfound astroresources. The samples will help illustrate how your knowledge comes beautifully together to give short and meaningful insights into a chart. By the time you finish this chapter, you will be well prepared to pick up any chart and highlight the main components yourself. Let's get started!

What Is a Birth Chart?

A birth chart, or natal chart, is a chart that is 360 degrees and divided into twelve equal parts, or houses, each of which is composed of thirty degrees. A birth chart provides detailed information about the sky and position of the signs and planets at the exact time of your birth. You will need to gather some important information to properly structure a chart, including the time, date, and location of your birth. With these, you can piece together your horoscope in the form of a birth chart. By doing so, you'll be able to create a road map that's relatively easy to follow.

Creating a birth chart can be as complicated as you make it, and you can leave out smaller elements, such as angles, aspects, asteroids, and comets to make things simple for yourself as you begin. Though you may notice some generational themes, your personal planets will be extremely meaningful and special to you as an individual. Let's take a closer look.

Reading and Interpreting Your Birth Chart

Let's look at the key components of your birth chart and how to begin to read and interpret them. It is suggested that you approach the below list of signs, houses, planets, and aspects in the order they are listed since each element builds on the others and adds levels of complexity to the chart. Remember to keep in mind that each of the signs and planets has a yin/yang and elemental quality as you seek to expand on your insights. Astrological fluency is really about your commitment to knowing all the disparate parts of a chart, including the various components, their glyphs, and how a zodiac wheel is structured. Having these pieces in place will ensure you're best able to easily intuit a logical and relevant story out of the parts.

Zodiac Signs

Within a horoscope wheel, the signs live within the outside rim of the chart. The signs are represented by their respective glyphs, so as you get familiar with these symbols, you'll start to recognize that readily reading the chart becomes easier. You'll notice that all the twelve signs are represented on the wheel, which means all of them are contained within each person's chart in their own way. They each represent various psychological impulses or needs. When you are first looking at a chart, it's best to locate the sun, moon, and ascendant signs first. Watch out for cusps, or signs that fall in between houses. Remember that the ascendant is always located on the left in the first house (where the sun rises) and that the signs always follow the same clockwise order around the zodiac, starting in Aries and ending with Pisces.

Houses

The "where" of the zodiac, the twelve houses, are sections that comprise a zodiac wheel. This will give you a glimpse as to which parts of your life have the most activity and astrological focus. These twelve sectors are fixed, meaning they show up in the same position in every chart. The houses are symbolic of different areas of your life. The first six houses are considered personal, addressing childhood to adolescence, and the last six deal with people and events in your community and adult life. Signs appear on the cusp of each house, depending on the time and place of your birth. The signs and planets revolve around the houses, just as the stars in the night sky appear to revolve around Earth.

Planets

The planets and essential luminaries, named after gods and goddesses from ancient pantheons, are archetypal in nature. They show up inside the houses, under a specific sign in a birth chart. Each of the planets represents a part of the psyche that is playing out its dramas in a certain fashion (signs), in a certain area of your life (houses). For example, Venus in the seventh house could indicate a particularly auspicious time for a love and partnership union. Chiron in the same house could indicate a karmic past around lovers and relationships. The sign the planet falls under gives the planet color and demonstrates the way it is activated. It's possible to have multiple planets under one sign or house in one chart. A stellium is when three or more planets fall under the same sign, creating an amplified effect for those planets.

Aspects

The aspects of astrology describe the relationships of the planets to one another in a chart. To calculate aspects, the planets and number of degrees between them are considered. You can see aspects in a chart represented by different color lines that connect, intersect, or oppose/square the planets. Since the planets have both favorable and disharmonious relationships to one another, knowing this bit of information can help identify tricky areas of your chart or forecast an upcoming opportunity. The aspects are the final dimension of chart reading covered by this book in this chapter, but they should be considered icing on the cake.

Angles and Aspects

Angels and aspects in a chart give new dimensions and depth to your readings by helping explain the relationships planets have to one another in a chart. Considering these components can help you refine your broad horoscope knowledge and present relevant key information to help you define relationships in your life, not just to people, but to things, places, and events. Although these details can often seem complicated and obscure, this section will help clear up any doubts you may have about using them for simple chart interpretations. You can feel free to leave these out of a reading but adding them may provide more relevance around transits and help you provide additional meaning to a basic horoscope chart.

Angles

There are four points in a chart that you'll want to keep your eye on.

Ascendant: Or rising-sign point, represents your surface-level personality or the mask that you wear in front of others. This is the side of you that others interact with the most.

Descendant: Is directly across from ascendant. Tells you what you seek in relationships with others and what attracts you.

Midheaven (MC): Stands high at the top of a chart and represents your professional success and public image. Think of this as the highest possible outcome, or your purpose for being here in this lifetime.

THE MOON'S PHASES

Lunar energy represents your subconscious mind and inner realm of emotions. It is often thought that shifting states and natural cycles mirror the moon's phases. The moon has eight phases per month, which repeat on a regular basis (approximately every 29.5 days). The four major phases of the moon are new, waxing, full, and waning, with four transitional moon phases laced in between.

The moon impacts your birth chart and therefore affects your unique astrological design. You can easily find a free lunar calculator online on almost any astrology website to determine the phase the moon was in at the time of your birth; you'll just need your natal information (date/time/location of birth) to do so.

The moon phase you were born under can reveal added intricate layers of who you are, including your emotional and subconscious operating systems. Which cycle were you born under? Which cycle do you feel you are in now? Exploring the moon's phases may help you connect the dots between your past, present, and future.

New: New beginnings, fresh starts, clarity, intention setting, planting seeds
Waxing Crescent/Gibbous: Motivation, momentum, creativity, seed grows to plant
First Quarter: Resistance and obstacles
Waxing Gibbous: Redirecting course, searching for truth
Full: Harvest, healing, charging, cleansing
Waning Gibbous: Gratitude, generosity, wisdom
Last Quarter: Release, letting go, forgiveness
Waning Crescent: Introspection, cycles ending, surrender, clearing

Imum Coeli (IC): Sits directly across from your MC at the bottom of your chart. The focus here is on your private, inner world.

If you draw lines between the four points, they create paths that form angles in your chart. Angles in a horoscope chart occur at intersections along the horizontal and vertical axes of a chart.

Aspects

Aspects in your chart refer to the angles the planets' positions create with each other and to other areas of interest within a birth chart. The aspects work together to form a relationship with each other. But like all relationships, each one is different. It's important to note that the aspects may have a neutral, harmonious, or tense relationship to one another. These areas in a birth chart reveal different areas in life where you may be thriving or struggling. The five major aspects are:

Sextiles: Positive angles that form when planets are 60 degrees apart in a chart.

Trines: Occur when planets are 120 degrees apart from one another, creating smooth connection. These are harmonious placements that help bring mutual stimulation to both placements.

Squares: Reveal problematic relationships and occur when planets square off to 90-degree angles in a chart.

Oppositions: Also reveal problematic relationships and occur when planets are 180 degrees directly across from one another.

Conjunctions: Can be charmed or disharmonious depending on the planets involved but can be generally considered neutral aspects. They occur when planets are 0 degrees away from one another, or intersecting. When you see a conjunction, you'll want to interpret this as a blend of the personality traits from each planet involved.

MINOR ASPECTS

There are five minor aspects in addition to the five major aspects in astrology. These are rather specific and beyond the scope of this book, however, because aspects can be viewed as vital information to color a chart, they are worth mentioning here, as they often show up in readings.

Quincunx (or Injunct): Occurs at 150 degrees between planets under different elements and modalities. This aspect makes it very difficult for common ground to be found and invites adjustment or redirection, as these planets will be incompatible by nature. Planets conflict when their differences are so complex that they are in complete discord, with no amount of integration being able to mend the gap.

Quintile: Occurs at 72 degrees, indicating a favorable creative talent or agency, and this is the one super-positive aspects of the minor aspects.

Semisextile: Found at 30 degrees, meaning the aspects are in adjacent signs. A semisextile is considered somewhat positive, as it can mean an opening for growth and evolution.

Semisquare: Located at 45 degrees. It is a half square, and like the square, it represents a block. This is a challenging aspect, and when this occurs in a chart, it can indicate frustration.

Sesquisquare: Occurs at 135 degrees, which is technically neutral, or a holding of breath. It can cause tension, but the choice is there for you to anchor into the highest frequency to surrender and grow.

Sample Birth Chart Readings

Now that you have a solid foundation on how to read the key components within a chart, let's look at some samples. These charts are unique and different, so approach each independently. Take an overall view of the whole chart at first, noticing things that jump out and then move to identifying the elements and modalities that are present. You may want to make a copy of the chart and write the details directly on the page, but many of the big astrology websites should include this information. Before you read the provided chart interpretations, try taking a stab at it on your own, and then go back and check your work. Happy reading!

Sample Birth Chart #1

When you look at the ascendant, you see this person is a Cancer rising, with a sun in Capricorn in the sixth house and moon in Libra in the fourth house. This tells you the person is a nurturer and deeply caring individual, with a focus on health and structure. The individual is likely a homebody, with a strong parental or maternal attachment, due to their moon placement. You see Venus in the fifth house in Sagittarius, which tells you the person is both fun loving and deeply romantic. You will also notice some interesting aspects here, particularly squares, oppositions, and trines. Opposition between the transpersonal planets and the personal planets can cause some conflict and struggle in the houses they fall under. You can see a trine between the moon/Mercury and moon/Pluto, boding well for these bodies in their respective houses.

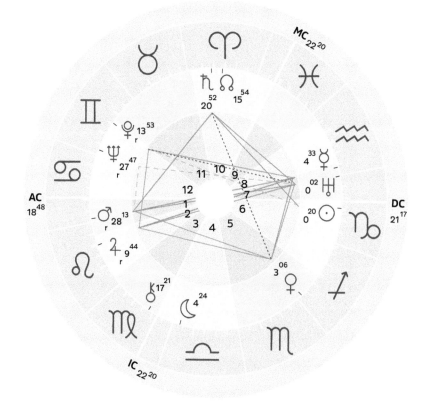

Sample Birth Chart #2

This person has an Aquarius ascendant in Aquarius (first house), sun in Taurus (third house), and moon in Libra (eighth house). With a sun in the third house, you can expect this person to excel in communication, and they may even write, act, or teach professionally. The individual has a well-developed mind, loves the outdoors, and has a strong affinity for self-care. Chiron in the third house indicates that the person could have had a past karmic relationship, which is now resolving through the way they create and communicate. The moon in the eighth house means the person would be quite accustomed to transition and change, and the ascendant indicates the person is here to help humanity. The fifth and seventh houses of dating, relationships, and marriage are empty, the interpretation could mean the person isn't focused on marriage or partnership. Leo rulership in the seventh would mean that the person prefers to flirt and have a good time, with no desire for a larger commitment until completely ready. You can also see the presences of another opposition, square, and trine here, as well as several conjunctions.

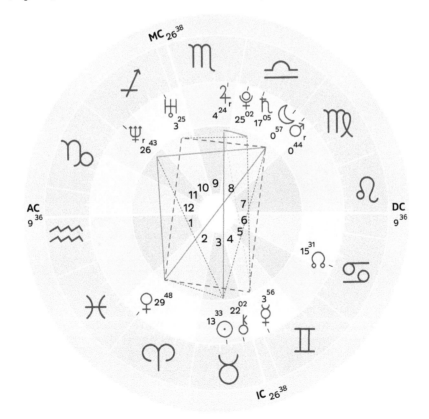

Sample Birth Chart #3

This chart shows a sun in Capricorn in the third house, moon in Aquarius in the third house, and ascendant in Scorpio in the first house. You'll notice much activity in the "Eastern" hemisphere of the chart, with the fourth, fifth, and seventh houses completely empty. Remember, when houses are empty, there isn't a ton of energy being played out there. With Mercury in the second house in Sagittarius, the person is witty, clever, and unafraid of their true expression. Hardworking and ambitious, this person gives back to their community. With an MC in Leo, this indicates someone in leadership who goes after their goals. Jupiter is in Gemini in the eighth house, so the person can expect investment opportunities with other people's money. You can also see some sextiles, trines, and conjunctions present as well.

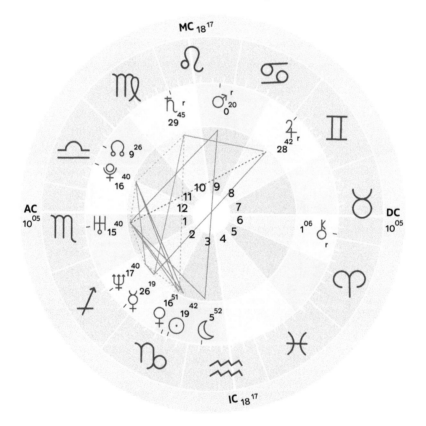

Key Takeaways

This chapter combined learning from the previous chapters to synthesize your knowledge. By analyzing three sample birth charts, you were able to put your newfound abilities to work. There was a lot in this chapter, so here's a little recap:

◆ Building a cohesive story is essential to creating meaning out of a zodiac chart. To do so, you'll need to combine as many of the big components as you are able to.

◆ You learned about aspects and angles, which are formed by the intersections of lines representing degrees that planets are separated by in a chart.

◆ There are five major and five minor aspects in a chart. It is suggested to learn the major aspects (conjunction, trine, opposition, sextile, square) and be able to identify them to add depth to your readings.

◆ The moon's phases represent your lunar emotional landscape and could be factored into a chart. You can use an online horoscope generator to identify the phase the moon was in at your birth, which is an indicator of your general temperament.

◆ You are so much more than your sun sign. All the signs are included in your natal chart, so keep this in mind as each sign and planet contributes to the whole unique picture of you.

CHAPTER EIGHT

Health and Self-Care

hile a birth chart can be a great indicator of various intimate details of your life, such as health, love, and work, it isn't able to tell you which paths to take. Those choices are up to you. However, the chart can give you some valuable insight, clarity, and direction as to what will best benefit you and help you become aware of what to pay attention to.

The next few chapters will focus on ways in which astrology plays out in different sectors of your personal life. This information can be used as a quick reference to effortlessly help with some on-the-go guidance. In this chapter, you will explore the role of health and self-care, how astrology plays a role in these areas, and what to look for in your birth chart to help your body function at its best. You'll start by looking beyond the sun sign and focus on relevant planets, houses, and signs for this matter. By considering chart placements and details, you can open up possibilities for yourself that you might not have known existed.

How Does Astrology Play a Role in Your Health and Self-Care?

You can learn a lot about how to best care for yourself by looking at your chart.

Astrology opens you up to new insights into all aspects of your life. While your birth chart won't give you exact answers, it can point you in the right direction and help you learn more about what you need, where you excel, and challenges you may face. You could learn what to expect from your body and how best to provide nurturing and nourishment.

Astrology can even be a tool that you use to help forecast the best possible time to start a new self-care routine. For example, you wouldn't want to plan any big changes or alter your routine during a Mercury retrograde since this is typically a time when you experience quirks and irregularities, either with technology, time, or both. A wise thing to do would be to wait, especially on creating binding contracts during any time that typical schedules or activities experience inversion, or a break from the norm. By using this type of simple forecasting, you can plan for a large event like a wedding or graduation party or plot the best time to start a new fitness class, begin a new nutrition plan, or even go to the spa. These details seem obscure but if you start to zoom out and look at the bigger picture, you can come up with an optimal time frame that feels cosmologically supported.

SELF-CARE 101

In the world of wellness, the term *self-care* gets thrown around quite a bit. I can tell you after working as a healer and Reiki master teacher for over ten years in Los Angeles, I have seen and heard of just about every self-care technique out there. There are so many areas in which you can give yourself loving attention and manage your own healing. Self-care can be physical, emotional, psychological, social, professional, financial, spiritual, and environmental, to name a few. Self-care can mean going on a walk, getting enough sleep, doing a digital detox, gratitude journaling, taking a bath, saying no, or creating boundaries. It can also mean asking for help when you need it, getting a life coach, meditating, decluttering your home, going on a retreat, or volunteering . . . the list goes on.

To know exactly what self-care is, you should also look at what it is not. Self-care is not loading more onto your plate when you really need to be hitting pause. It is not distracting yourself with busywork to avoid dealing with your essential needs. Nor is it creating an emergency plan for imminent burnout. The goal is to proactively foster healthy habits and behaviors to avoid burnout in the first place. If you are already in that place, learn to recognize it, and be real with yourself on planning to course correct. Because above all, self-care isn't being selfish. Self-care is making sure you are living your best life in alignment with your own beautiful gifts that you get to share with the world when you have a full cup of your own to give from.

Significant Health Houses

When you're exploring health, wellness, and self-care within a chart, you can turn to specific houses for answers. You'll want to begin by researching any planets and signs that fall within these "health" houses and planets that have aspects to these houses. If two or more signs fall within these houses, you'll want to read and interpret for each. Take note of your sign ruling that house and determine the general energy of the sign. For example, is it day (yang) or night (yin). As an example, Taurus here can mean a slow and steady approach to fitness, but its ruler Venus may indicate issues with blood sugar, as Venus likes sweetness and comfort. You'll want to

HEALING MODALITIES

You learned earlier about the idea of self-care, what it is, and what it is not. Let's expand a bit here by learning about a few practices that fall under physical, emotional, and spiritual self-care. These are specific practices you can seek out to help improve your well-being and heal yourself from the inside out.

One of my most beloved healing practices, which I highly recommend, is Reiki. This is a gentle hands-on or remote healing that involves energy channeling to move ki within the body and aura. Ki, or chi, is life-force energy that can sometimes become blocked, causing physical, emotional, or spiritual distress. With the help of a Reiki practitioner, you can balance your chakras and unblock the energy centers, leading to a more balanced life. Another beautiful practice is acupuncture. This is a TCM (traditional Chinese medicine) practice that uses small needles to help move the ki through the meridian lines within the physical body.

Another great healing practice is yoga. Though it is a movement practice, it is also a way of life. By studying yoga, you can learn about the eight limbs and put them into practice in your life for more fulfillment. The eight limbs are: yamas (attitudes toward the environment), niyamas (attitudes toward ourselves), asana (physical postures/movement), pranayama (breathwork), pratyahara (sensory limitation), dharana (concentration), dhyana (meditation), and samadhi (enlightenment/integration). If you're looking to practice the asanas and move your body, you can always try a new style of yoga, like ashtanga, yin, or hot yoga, to mix things up a bit.

investigate medical astrology to start to find all the medical-related issues by planet and sign, as each has its own specific associations. The houses that most influence your health are the fourth, sixth, eighth, and twelfth. The sixth house is the big one that you would look at first because it's the house of health (and work). Here you can find general physical health, revealing your body's natural temperament, physiology, health, and physique. Next, look to the fourth house, to dive into how to best nurture the body since this house is ruled by the moon. This home will also apply to mothering/nurturing, emotional needs, and mental health. In the eighth house, you find matters of sex and sexuality. This can illuminate areas of codependency, sexual trauma, and physical and emotional effects of these things in one's life. The twelfth house is another secondary place to look for emotional and mental health, as this house reveals all that is normally concealed in the unconscious and dream states.

Health and Self-Care for Your Sun Sign

This section will give you an idea of how you generally think of health and work it into your daily life. Your well-being matters, and each unique sign behaves differently and has distinct ways of managing and caring for their own health.

Most people mainly use their sun sign to better understand themselves, so you can begin by referencing your sun sign below, though you are far more than your sun sign alone. It is also a good idea to look up your ascendant sign from these lists so you can get another point of reference when you are thinking about your holistic health as a complete story.

Aries

These individuals have contagious enthusiasm, high-spirited energy, endurance, and strength due to Mars rulership in this sign. They will need to watch out for overdoing it, as issues here stem from stress and packing too much into their schedule. They may be prone to impatience and frustration, especially when others aren't keeping up. Aries natives tend to stay active and usually have a solid constitution.

Aries rules the head and energy levels. Look out for headaches, brain fog, or migraines as a sign to slow down. Issues related to the head, face, facial muscles, and eyes may appear here. Rams are highly motivated characters who enjoy a good competition. To cool down, meditation is recommended. Nutritionally, protein, lipids, and lots of omega-3, omega-6, and omega-9 fatty acids will help keep the physical form and mental states satisfied.

Taurus

Taurus loves a good cozy nap more than anyone, so expect this sign to be into resting. They enjoy comfort foods, and with a Venus rulership, this means they may crave sugar more than most. Nutritionally, they benefit from iodine-rich foods, like seaweed, shrimp, sesame seeds, and garlic. They can supplement their diet with kelp and various vitamins, like vitamin A and C, selenium, zinc, and copper.

Taurus is associated with the neck and shoulders. This includes the tongue, tonsils, jaw, thyroid, larynx, chin, and ears. The throat here is shared with Gemini rulership. Issues that may arise here include TMJ, thyroid problems, tonsilitis, or earaches and infections. Bulls may also be prone to losing their voice. They are known to have great upper-body strength.

Gemini

Gemini is best known for its link to the lungs (air element) and breath. It also rules the arms, elbows, and wrists (but not the hands). The upper rib cage, shoulders, bronchial tubes, and thymus are associated here as well and sometimes the throat (shared with Taurus). Closely tied into all these parts is the nervous system, also governed by Gemini. Natives here tend to be overactive and should take precautions to move more slowly to avoid injuries. Mercurial rulership here means issues may stem from communication or throat-related problems.

Due to their naturally busy lifestyles, Geminis benefit from healthy food on the go, such as wraps and smoothies. Nutritionally, they need cayenne, lemon, ginger, and omega-3. Fruit and protein are also excellent choices here.

Cancer

Cancer is ruler of the midsection. This includes the chest, breasts, stomach, and upper digestive system, lower rib cage, and pancreas. Because the crab and the moon are highly linked with femininity and yin energy, the womb and uterus fall under Cancer. Native Cancers may be prone to stomachaches, as they internalize stress. They need to find healthy ways to release stress, or this could result in disrupted sleep patterns.

Like Taurus, crabs go after comfort foods. They need to be mindful not to overdo emotional eating. Incorporating cruciferous vegetables, like cauliflower, broccoli, kale, Brussels sprouts, and cabbage, can help with digestion, as well as kimchi and kombucha or other lightly fermented foods.

Leo

The heart and upper back are ruled by Leo. This includes the scapula, spleen, spine, and aorta. Protecting health and the cardiovascular system through exercise and proper diet are important, as well as tending to matters of the heart. Leos should focus on keeping the heart open and loving without expectation of anything in return. They must be mindful to monitor their egos to make sure they are not overinflated. With sun rulership, these folks should take care to wear sunscreen to protect against melanoma.

As a fire sign, these lions enjoy spicy food of all types. They enjoy gourmet foods but may need to stay away from foods too rich in fat to aid in their heart health. Supplements for Leos include hawthorn berry, cacao, folate, pomegranate, vitamin D, and coenzyme Q10.

Virgo

Virgos rule over the abdomen, lower digestive tract, and sympathetic nervous system, which connects the internal organs to the nerves in the spine. When the sympathetic nervous system is activated, it helps prepare an organism for stress by bringing blood flow to the skin. This is the fight-or-flight response, associated with Virgos. These folks should be cautious not to allow their repressed anxiety to get the best of them, as this could lead to irritable bowel syndrome (IBS), inflammation, and bloating.

Expect this sign to be the meal preppers of the zodiac. Unprocessed whole foods are best for them, like spinach, lettuce, leafy greens, lentils, and brown rice. Fruits and veggies containing potassium are best for them, including bananas, beans, raisins, avocado, and winter squash.

Libra

Libra rules the lower back and spine, specifically the lumbar region. The kidneys are included here, as well as the adrenal glands and skin, the body's largest organ. With a Venusian ruler, they should be wary of sugars but can supplement with agave or low-glycemic index natural sweeteners. Libras benefit from paying attention to how they feel on the inside, rather than how they look on the outside. These folks should take care not to stress their adrenals by avoiding high-impact exercise as well as caffeine. Getting lots of sleep assists this Venusian with their beauty rest.

Unprocessed foods that help support proper kidney function and repair include apples, blueberries, kale, sweet potatoes, and fish. Supplements for Libras include essential fatty acids; magnesium; zinc; selenium; vitamins B5, C, D, and E; antioxidants; ashwagandha; collagen; and peptides.

Scorpio

Scorpio rules over the hips and reproductive systems. This includes the cervix, prostate, bladder, and the urinary tract. Keeping in mind that the womb is associated with Cancer signs, Scorpio rules over the genitals, so disease can manifest there. Plutonian rulership here indicates a need for precaution and discernment regarding healthy sexual partners. Hip-opening exercises are best for this group, as well as routine self-care.

Scorpios love food, often displaying their passion through their food choices. Good food choices include asparagus, radishes, cauliflower, and figs. Supplements for Scorpios include folic acid, calcium, vitamins E and D, fish oils, coenzyme Q10 and selenium, probiotics, L-arginine, and flaxseed.

Sagittarius

Sagittarius rules the thighs, legs, pelvis, and liver. They should take care to guard against injury to these areas. With a Jupiter ruler, this sign needs to be mindful they don't overdo it, since injuries can result when the body is pushed beyond its limits. Make sure to get enough rest, Sagittarius, as this is your body's main recovery tool.

Native Sagittarius enjoy food as they do travel—as much variety as they can get their hands on. This fire sign has a penchant for spice and will need to take a cool-down break for their digestive benefit from time to time. This sign needs to keep moderation in mind and get enough protein. Keep the liver cleansed with lemons, limes, turmeric, beets, ginger, carrots, and milk thistle extract.

Capricorn

Capricorn rules the skeletal system. This includes the bones, joints, and teeth. Capricorns should take care to guard against injury to the bones, especially as they age, since mature bones are more brittle. Proper dental care for Capricorns is highly advised, especially if the mouth holds metal fillings.

Practical diets and simple foods are what a Capricorn craves, but don't be fooled, they also love to go gourmet. They enjoy dining out with friends and displaying their love of extravagant food. Vegetables that ground and connect them to earth are best, including root veggies, like beets, carrots, and potatoes. Dairy also works for this sign, as it is an excellent source of vitamin D. Nutritionally, they need calcium, magnesium, and potassium for strong bone health.

Aquarius

Aquarius rules over the ankles and circulatory system. This includes the heels, shins, and calves. Athletes and yogis may want to get a good preworkout stretch in to ensure proper flexibility. They should consider wrapping their ankles and taking plenty of rest to prevent injuries, as they are prone to them. Though the nervous system is ruled by Gemini, it also holds an association here and shared links through Uranus, ruler of Aquarius. Stress-reduction techniques, like meditation, are highly recommended.

As an air sign, these folks need food to fuel their active minds. Cordyceps, chaga, MCT oil, and ginkgo biloba are great supplements for this sign. Brain foods include spinach, celery, butternut squash, and chicken. Nutrition with little fat will do their bodies good.

Pisces

Pisces rules the hands and feet as well as the immune system. This sign needs routine pampering through massage, nail care, energy work, and rest. Lymph care such as specific lymph drainage massage or yoga postures to increase lymph flow are suggested. Like fish in the sea, movement (dance) and water (baths) are good for the well-being of Pisces.

Since these natives can hold unconscious patterning easily and tend to be natural empaths, they may tend to feel a lot on behalf of others. Emotional cleansing through daily journaling is highly recommended. Pisces food choices should include iron-rich foods, like beans, steamed veggies, parsley, garlic, and fresh fruits. They should take care to build their immune system with supplements like zinc, vitamin C, and elderberry.

Key Takeaways

There is so much a birth chart can show you about your health. Here is a recap of this chapter, which can help you make the most of your self-care practices to increase energy and well-being.

- ◆ Astrology can be a tool that you use to help forecast the best possible time to plan a procedure, what to expect from your body, and how best to provide nurturing and nourishment.

- ◆ Each sign rules a different area of the body, as well as has varied nutritional needs, dietary concerns, and physical areas of focus.

- ◆ Self-care isn't selfish. Self-care involves taking care of your physical, emotional, psychological, and spiritual needs to ensure that you aren't putting yourself last.

- ◆ Certain houses in your chart have a pronounced effect on your health. These houses are the fourth and sixth (primary) and eighth and twelfth (secondary).

- ◆ There are many natural healing modalities that can assist with general health improvements on a physical, emotional, and spiritual level, including Reiki, acupuncture, and yoga as a way of life.

CHAPTER NINE

Relationships and Romance

hen it comes to romance, you want to make sure you're aligning with someone who has a reasonable amount of compatibility with you and the ability to grow and evolve as your relationship matures. Astrology can give you a road map to better relationships of all kinds. You can also recognize your soul mates through a deeper look at your charts together, called a synastry chart. Your soul mates include your lovers, partners, friends, and others who are intimately linked to you. After all, your entire life is about building relationships, so by understanding your relationship blueprints with others, you'll be best equipped to manage them long-term.

In this chapter, you'll look at how astrology impacts your relationships and love life by going through the signs' "love personalities." You'll explore chart synastry, what nodes mean for romance, and significant house relationships that deal with love. You'll also look at each sign's "best fit" and explore common needs and desires. With this invaluable information, you'll be able to reach your ultimate goals in love and personal relationships.

How Does Astrology Impact Your Relationships and Romance?

Since astrology provides insights into all aspects of your life, you can learn a lot about how you show up in relationships and romantic partnerships by looking at your birth chart. While your birth chart won't give you exact answers, it can point you in the right direction and help you learn more about what you need, where you excel, and what challenges or pitfalls you may face in this area. Astrology can illuminate a potential or current partner's patterns and tendencies so you can be better prepared to manage the relationship. By looking at the natal chart, you can determine who you'll naturally be a great fit with for romance and more. You can tell how someone may lean when it comes to kids, partnership, and marriage.

You will need to keep in mind that elements and aspects can help you add color into the reading to determine compatibility. This chapter will be focused on the sun signs and how they behave in a romantic dynamic, though when it comes to love, there is so much more within a chart that creates a full picture. Be sure to take into consideration the elements of each sign, as they play a key role in compatibility. For example, fire loves fire and needs air to survive but doesn't typically mix well with water or earth. As always, take what resonates and leave the rest. Be willing and open to explore your own patterns that might be limiting you and willing to give chances beyond who the birth chart says is the right fit. Everyone has baggage, and no one is perfect. There may be a suggested fit astrologically speaking that doesn't work out or another sign you hadn't considered that is perfect for you when you take more than a sun sign into account.

CHART SYNASTRY

Chart synastry is the astrology of relationships. A synastry chart compares the relationships of two people by layering their individual charts on top of one another. To obtain a synastry chart, you'll need the birth chart information for each person. You can then compare certain markers between the charts to assess compatibility. A synastry chart is much more nuanced than a single sun sign will be as an indicator of your love-match potential.

For example, you may choose to look at one another's suns and moons, Venus placements, and seventh-house planets. The benefit here is that you'll be showcasing the best possible perspective of each person's qualities when it comes to love. Keep in mind that a synastry report doesn't predict the path of a relationship but merely gives you guideposts as a blueprint of what's possible in best-case outcomes. Remember that a relationship that is astrologically amazing on paper may not be what you experience in real life. There is an endless array of outcomes, based on personal life experience, social background, and other factors. The outcome of your relationship with someone will always be determined by you and them.

Significant Relationship Houses, Planets, and More

The big houses to look at when considering relationships in your life are the fifth, seventh, and eighth houses. In general, to find the tension in a chart, you'll want to look at any aspects to planets Saturn, Pluto, and Neptune. These oppositions, squares, and other areas of tension could suggest anxiety, blocks, and inhibitions around expression of love. In general, you'll want to find the Venus placement in a chart to determine the general outlook on love.

In the fifth house lives sex, pleasure, and desire. This is a house of happiness, and it's here that you'll notice your style of giving love to others. For example, sun/Leo in the fifth house denotes giving love through authentic expression, creativity, and sharing humor, while a moon/Cancer placement points to giving love through nurturing behaviors and sharing emotions freely.

The seventh house defines how you pair up, both romantically and otherwise, including business relationships and friendships. It's natural to look here to get a good idea of what your highest potential holds. Though it's termed the house of marriage, you don't need planets in this house to have a relationship last forever or to be legally married to someone at all. This is simply a place that dictates your natural tendencies toward self-orientation and/or partner orientation.

The eighth house looks at love from a passionate lens. This is where love takes a deeper meaning through sexual love, which is intimate and sacred. It is the merging of two lives into one and the mysteries that relationship brings. Planets here will be a strong indicator of the force of attraction that keeps you together.

NODES: KARMA AND DHARMA

There are two moon nodes that are looked at in astrology. These are the north and south nodes, representing the two points where the moon's orbit intersects with the ecliptic. The moon crosses in a northerly direction and then a southernly direction, creating the nodes from an earthly perspective. They are always opposing one another and will never meet. In some cultures, this is known as a dragon line, and these node connections exist within personal astrology, but also on the chakras of the earth itself, through the ley lines around the world. They symbolize a path of emotional and spiritual development for one's soul evolution and I refer to them as your karma and dharma points on a chart. *Karma* being the past (your past lifetimes, habits, patterns, as well as early life in your current incarnation), and *dharma* being your future soul's potential. Together these nodes signal a continuum of development with neither node being all bad or all good. These are indicators of your self-actualized growth. By looking at the houses and signs your nodes fall under, you can predict where you have come from and where you are going, in life, love, and every area in between.

Romance and Relationships
for Your Sun Sign

This section will provide specific advice on romance and relationships for each of the twelve signs. By using these as general guides, you can use the information below to consciously create, mend, or boost a romantic relationship in your life. The best part is that this part won't require a full natal chart from your partner's end. If you know their birthday, you'll be able to sort their sun sign on your own. Take a sincere look at your own qualities that you bring to the table, and then measure them up against what you are seeking or desiring in the romance department. Remember to keep in mind that astrology is used as a predictive tool; it cannot predict the efficacy of a real-life relationship. Leave room for surprises when considering matters of the heart, and you won't be disappointed.

Aries

Bold Aries goes after what they want in love, making them an admirable pursuer.

This enthusiastic fire sign will always let you know where you stand, and you'll never need to question their desire. These individuals are direct as can be and are often the initiators in a relationship. To passive signs, this may come off as intimidating and a bit overwhelming. This sign appreciates differences and respects their partner, often showing interest in their partner's passions as a pledge of loving endearment. Aries natives prefer activity in their love lives and a partner who takes care of themselves in health and fitness. This sign pairs best with other fire signs (Leo and Sagittarius) and air signs (Aquarius, Gemini, and Libra).

Taurus

Loyal beyond measure, Taurus will take their time committing in a romantic relationship. This grounded sign will make sure they are totally certain before starting something serious. Their sense of stability, family, and finances make them excellent long-term partners. These individuals are down to earth and patient, though they can tend to be a little stubborn. Once you cross them, beware, as this sign doesn't forgive easily. These natives bring a devotional love that adores both their partner and the finer things that love and life have to offer. They naturally crave the good life, so if their partner can cook and tidy a home, consider it a done deal. Taurus pairs best with other earth signs (Virgo and Capricorn) and water signs (Cancer, Scorpio, and Pisces).

Gemini

Gemini is diverse and requires variety in a relationship. This means be willing to grow and go on new adventures if you're dating this sign. Flirtatious and fast to fall in love, this sign craves intellectual conversations and someone to keep up with their quick-witted humor. Though they desire chemistry, this sign is likely to be best friends with their love. It's important that their partner be a listener, as this will add to their charm for talkative Gemini. Debate skills are a plus, but it's also necessary for Gemini's partner to be tolerant of Gemini keeping lots of friends around. This sign pairs best with other breezy air signs (Aquarius and Libra) and bold fire signs (Aries, Leo, and Sagittarius).

Cancer

Caring and sensitive, Cancers fall in love hard once they've entered the realm of romance. This sign isn't the type to take dating lightly, as they are more likely to get caught up in the search for the One than having a variety of partners. Crabs are highly committed and devoted partners and take pride in nurturing and caring for partners, children, and home matters. Conversations are easy to have once you get them to open up, as they share their feelings freely. Cancers can be rather guarded and overly cautious, though, if they don't trust you for any reason. Cancer pairs best with other sensitive water signs, like Pisces and Scorpio, and grounded and consistent earth signs like Virgo, Capricorn, and Taurus.

Leo

Leo's radiant fire can cause romantic sparks to ignite quickly, though they will want to see consistency before they commit to you. Be sure to show up and wait on the invitation for more. They'll be the first to show you the green light. Once past the dating phase, long-term relationship Leos will be enthusiastic, inventive, and expressive. This is a bold sign, but they prefer not to argue. They do not mind having off-the-cuff discussions and sharing their big heart with you and your inner circle. Lions are highly passionate individuals, while enjoying a cool persona in public. Though this sign loves to have fun, don't ever make fun of your lion, as this is generally a big no-no. Lions pair best with other fire signs (Sagittarius and Aries) and air signs (Aquarius, Gemini, and Libra).

Virgo

Virgos tend to be relationship stewards, serving their relationship needs well. Their approach to dating is conservative, and they prefer to be wooed intellectually, often waiting for you to make the first move. This sign is impressed by preparation and well-thought-out planning, and shows their love through acts of service. Virgos thrive when attending to details, making plans, setting up travel, arranging reservations, and visioning the future, so they make excellent long-term partners. These individuals are down to earth and extraordinarily reliable. Though it seems demanding, they only hold you to the highest standard because they believe in you and want you to be the best you possible. Virgos possess a sensual and passionate side, on their terms. Virgos pair best with other earth signs (Taurus and Capricorn) and water signs (Scorpio, Pisces, and Cancer).

Libra

Libras, ruled by Venus, crave love, beauty, style, and comfort. They are charming, seductive, giving, and affectionate. They need someone who can support their need for socializing and keeping lots of friends around. If you are to be Libra's partner, you'll need to sparkle on all levels, as they are very picky as to who they surround themselves with. Because this sign has a judgmental mind, they can always see both sides to a situation and are not swayed by irrational or selfish behavior. Libras cherish and adore their partners. They are seen as open and inventive in the bedroom, so they will keep you on your toes. Fun-loving Libras go best with other air signs (Aquarius and Gemini) and fire signs (Sagittarius, Aries, and Leo).

Scorpio

Falling in love with this sign can be an addictive experience. Scorpios are passionate, mysterious, and intriguing, and seduction is their specialty. They are known to weave you slowly and deliberately into their enchanted web. You may find that your love is purposefully being kept a secret—this is completely normal for Scorpio. Scorpio lovers are devoted, loyal, and intense, so if you're the object of their desire, they'll want to go deep fast. Though some may call it obsession, they see it as desired willingness to explore true intimacy. Beware, though. If you cross this sign, they are known for dramatic, volcanic explosions. This sign clashes big-time with fire signs but meshes well with other water signs (Cancer and Pisces) and earth signs (Capricorn, Taurus, and Virgo).

Sagittarius

Filled with enthusiasm and fun, the good-humored and loving Sagittarius are quite affectionate and passionate lovers. This sign delights in the many pleasures in life and will want to mix things up, often by exploring new realms. They love to try new activities and traveling is a must for them. Keeping their interest may be a challenge since they demand someone with dynamic ambition and drive. Ever the philosopher, you'll also need to keep your Sagittarius entertained and engaged with intellectual conversation or new music/studies/programs you can participate in together. Sagittarius is energetic, strong-willed, and adventurous, with a zest for life that is almost unparalleled in the zodiac. They pair best with other fire signs (Aries and Leo) and air signs (Aquarius, Gemini, and Libra).

Capricorn

Preferring serious long-term partnerships over superficial brief encounters, Capricorns make dedicated and devoted partners. This sign has a shrewd to-the-point outlook on love and romance and will want to be friends first. Preferring to be efficient in all areas, they use their energy very selectively and deliberately when dating and getting to know you. This can be a slow process, and their manner of affection can be misunderstood, as they often come across as emotionally distant. This sign loves the finer things in life, so expect extravagant dinners and entertainment in style, though they are pragmatic and financially discerning enough to accomplish this with a level of controlled practicality. This stable and dedicated sign pairs best with other earth signs (Taurus and Virgo) and water signs (Cancer, Scorpio, and Pisces).

Aquarius

Aquarian lovers are spontaneous and enjoy a good time without much commitment. They can come off as detached and will want to avoid relationship labels while they get to know you. Enjoyable activities for them include activism, environment cleanup days, and volunteer work in which they can give back to their community. This lover can be known to hold intellectual conversation for hours, and their innate self-confidence is alluring and magnetic to others. Once an Aquarian decides you are the One, they are extremely dedicated partners. Beware, as this sign can be reactionary, and their wrath is swift and severe. They prefer to keep things light, calm, and cool whenever possible. This sign pairs best with other air signs (Gemini and Libra) and fire signs (Aries, Leo, and Sagittarius).

Pisces

Pisces are sensitive souls that require highly empathetic and spiritually oriented partners in love. In return, expect them to love and cherish you indefinitely. This sign takes pride in making you feel like you are on a pedestal. Piscean people can often find themselves hurt inside a romantic container because they are so gentle and fragile that they tend to bruise easily. They will require plenty of space to experience their feelings, which includes expressions like crying often, dancing in the rain, and taking endless bubble baths. This sign needs a creative match, and someone who doesn't mind merging lives and hearts. Pisces will need you to help them balance their inner world of emotions with a practical and grounded approach. This sign pairs best with other water signs (Cancer and Scorpio) and earth signs (Capricorn, Taurus, and Virgo).

Key Takeaways

By looking at the love style each sign portrays, you'll be better able to understand and communicate effectively with your partner. Before starting a romantic relationship, you may want to get an idea of their needs and your compatibility together. Key points within this chapter include:

♦ Elements and aspects can be a great indicator of relationship compatibility.

♦ A synastry chart is a tool that overlays two charts on top of one another to determine romantic compatibility. It's extremely helpful to use a synastry chart to gain a closer look at the aspects and planetary placements in each person's chart.

♦ The moon's nodes in a chart represent your past and your future, respectively. This is a good place to look to gain insight on past patterns and future goals within your relationship and personal chart.

♦ The big houses to look at when considering relationships in your life are the fifth, seventh, and eighth houses. To find the tension in a chart, look at any aspects to the planets Saturn, Pluto, and Neptune.

♦ Signs with the same element or a complementary element tend to make the best friends and partners because they naturally get along, though different pairings are possible, with some extra attention and awareness to each party's sensitivities.

CHAPTER TEN

Work and Career

Your aspirations, unique abilities, and raw talents all contribute to fulfilling your life. Becoming inspired by your passions and allowing them to guide you to your purpose take time, and astrology can help. Your birth chart can speak volumes about which direction might best serve your career journey and have the most impact. Allowing astrology to be a springboard for new ideas and motivation will help you by providing ideas on the choices you could make. Consider using the information provided in this chapter as suggestions for exciting new possibilities.

This chapter will present opportunities for you to explore optimal career choices and will present a bit more information about the MC/IC points in your chart. You'll get to know what this means in terms of your highest expression and how this connects to your ambitions. There will also be an exploration of each sign as it relates to strengths and drawbacks you might experience along the way to enable you to make empowered choices regarding your future endeavors. Finally, you will look at how eclipses influence cycles on earth and what happens when they occur. Eclipse times are ripe for growth, which ultimately leads to big change. To find out how this impacts your energy and more, let's dive in.

How Does Astrology Impact Your Work and Career?

You can learn a lot about how you show up for your work, career, and other professional goals by looking at your birth chart. You can even run a birth chart for your business to see the energy dynamics playing out there (along with other fun details, like the theme of your company's mission or when is an opportunistic time to buy/sell). While your personal birth chart can't give you exact answers, it can direct you to learn more about what you need, where you excel, and hurdles you may face in this area.

To get an idea about the work that would suit you best, remember that you are much more than your sun sign alone. Think of your full birth chart as a map that can highlight predictable paths of success, achievements, and even promotion prospects for a job. These astrological insights work best when paired with an open mind and perseverance. They will tell you how you shine best and how you might progress in the career path you choose, but ultimately it is up to you to stay in alignment with your natural abilities and what excites you most. Keep an open mind when looking at the suggestions below, and remember that if what you're doing for work sparks joy in you, you can't go wrong.

MIDHEAVEN AND IMUM COELI

Your midheaven (MC) and Imum Coeli (IC) are angles in astrology. The midheaven sits on the cusp of the tenth house, which is an indicator of long-term goals and career prospects. The midheaven, also known as the "middle sky" in Latin, is the highest place on your chart. Here you can get a glimpse of what your highest expression and service contributions are. This is a place to look at to determine goal setting and soul strategy. Ideally, this would also represent your career, though they don't always line up perfectly. Your MC also represents social standing and reputation. Get a look at the sign that rules your MC to learn more about your personal best self.

Your IC line sits directly opposite your MC. This is the lowest place on your chart, also known as the nadir. This is the area that represents your inner, private life. It rests on the cusp of the fourth house and can also symbolize your parents and your childhood home. This can be indicative of the foundations you set out with early in life and will paint a picture of what you need to be happy from the inside out.

Significant Houses and Aspects for Work and Career

Though this chapter will provide some invitations on how you might approach your purpose-driven work, alignment comes when you take your whole chart into consideration. For example, you might also want to include chart analysis from the sixth house to compare what type of work would fit your personality best or what your daily routine should look like. The tenth house is another place you'll want to check out when looking at your work-life balance because it represents long-term goals, public image, and fame. For example, Pluto transiting this section of your chart could mean a rebirth, uprooting, or reset of the foundations you once knew. Jupiter transiting would mean abundance and opportunities.

You'd also want to look at the placement of the midheaven point (MC) on the tenth house, and which sign it falls on, to receive a fuller picture of where you'll excel naturally. This line is where you aspire toward during your life.

Nodes are how your highest self works best in this life. Look at your dharma point or north node to get a feel for what purpose work would interest you. Make sure to note which sign and house it falls under. For example, a north node in Aries would tell you that you're the type to work on your own or be a leader in some way. This could mean entrepreneurship or running your own small business best fits your personality. There are many interpretations for each of these, so make sure to zoom out to view them all together for optimal results.

ECLIPSES

If you've ever heard someone cringe at the thought of eclipse season, you're not alone.

Eclipses, for better or for worse, are known to be harbingers of great change. This means that they bring fast endings, unexpected shifts, and rapid timeline dissolution. Expect transition and transformation during these periods. Eclipse phenomena usually occur in sets of three to six throughout the year, creating bookends around intense periods of change. Of course, any eclipse also can shake up your world in a good way, too. Don't forget these could be gateway opportunities to welcome new blessings, like engagements, babies, and other fun surprises.

There are several eclipses that matter in astrology, called lunar and solar eclipses. This is where the earth passes between the moon and the sun, or the moon passes between the earth and the sun. Think about these times as dynamic cosmic occurrences that can shift realities. Solar eclipses occur on new moons and often bring new beginnings and fresh starts, and open you to new energy. Lunar eclipses occur on full moons and usually bring major chapters to an end, revelations, and turning points. Both types of eclipses are game changers that require your full presence and conscious awareness to manage successfully.

Work and Career for Your Sun Sign

Your sun sign is an excellent indicator of work and personality compatibility. Use your passions to fuel your exploration and remember that each of the career suggestions available below are simply to be used as an inspirational jumping-off point. Since we are made up of every sign within us, it could provide a fuller picture to take a glimpse at your moon sign below as well and see how it compares to your sun sign alone. Remember sun signs will show you how you shine outward into the world, while moon signs for career will be satisfying to your inner world. Share these with family and friends and see how the results compare from person to person. Take the advice that resonates, and, as always, leave the rest.

Aries

With a ruler in Mars, Aries folks are usually insistent on getting their way and succeeding at anything they put their minds to. This sign is best suited to careers in which they take the lead and work independently. Aries thrives in fast-paced, demanding environments, and they are always up for challenges, making them tirelessly committed workers. Aries are constantly making decisions and handing out orders but rarely tolerate misunderstanding or insubordination. These individuals approach work fearlessly and pragmatically, which helps inspire those around them, though collaboration isn't really for them unless you let them take charge. You'll find many dynamic jobs that would suit an Aries, such as entrepreneur, military, law enforcement, EMT, firefighter, venture capitalist, fitness instructor, personal trainer, athlete, mechanic, chef, and tour guide.

Taurus

Taurus is dedicated, trustworthy, and dependable. These folks are hardworking and reliable, though procrastination can sometimes seep in. If you aren't in a rush to get the job done, Taurus will make sure to do the job carefully and right the first time. This sign's personality might be described as bossy to some, but only because they aren't ones to shirk responsibility. If delegation is called for, they are concerned with executing the instructions in a well-directed manner and aren't thrown for a loop during crisis. They prefer stability and security in the workplace. Jobs in the material-world realm make a good match for Taurus, such as florist, landscaper, real estate agent or broker, banker, stockbroker, mortgage officer, jeweler or craftsman, photographer, restaurant manager, and chef.

Gemini

Gemini's mercurial nature lends them to careers that provide lots of opportunity for them to sparkle, shine, and expand their awareness as they meet new people. This sign prefers a dynamic environment and loathes routine. Because Geminis are great speakers and enjoy multitasking, they thrive in a brisk, fast-paced workplace. These types are constantly on the move and tend to be restless and unpredictable in nature, so multiple side jobs or career changes during a lifetime are normal for them. They work best when they can delegate paperwork, which leaves the visioning and idea generating for them to handle on their own. Jobs for Geminis include journalist, editor, writer, advertising agent, creative director, engineer, teacher, communications specialist, film producer, entertainer, interpreter, TV host, salesperson, and personal assistant.

Cancer

Cancers make amazing caregivers and nurturers and can flourish in low-key and harmonious work environments. This sign will often be found deep in their own thought process and can get very absorbed by work. With a strict work ethic, Cancers are devoted workers. They should take care to maintain a work-life balance because they can be quite thrown off when their home-life balance is disturbed. Occasionally, coworkers may mistake Cancer for being withdrawn, moody, or distant, but this is just their private side acting reclusive. Emotional connection to their purpose work is important for them, and they tend to be good at handling finances. Job suggestions for this sign include doctor, nurse, pediatrician, counselor, teacher, accountant, business manager, real estate agent, interior designer, nutritionist, dietician, veterinarian, teacher, chef, social worker, or website designer.

Leo

Leo's biggest strength is being a compassionate leader. Directing from the heart, Leo is a master at orchestrating a crowd. The lion is fair, friendly, committed, and ambitious. These folks know how to take command, and they tend to assume top positions within companies or businesses. This sign is known to be fair and benevolent, guiding others from a place of love and altruism. They take pride in all they do. As an employee, Leo will need positive encouragement and attention. Loyal at their core, lions are above all dependable. This sign enjoys creativity, play, and entertainment, and they don't mind being in positions where they can really showcase their enormous light. Careers that light up Leos include acting, broadcasting, TV personality, comedy, modeling, child care provider, artist, and sales executive.

Virgo

Virgos are analytical and pragmatic, but above all, crave organization. This highly realist sign takes any job seriously and commits a high level of professionalism and honesty to their duties. They can be the most private people, so from the outside this may seem as though Virgo coworkers are modest and unassuming, yet they are simply hard at work. Most choose to separate work and play, so they may not make many friends inside office walls. They prefer to be in service to others, are highly detail oriented, and may tend to micromanage a task so things can be done to their standards. Jobs Virgos may like include copy editing, computer programming, upper management, accounting, data analyst, nutritionist, engineer, psychologist, psychiatrist, bank clerk, scientist, researcher, inspector, or receptionist.

Libra

Libras are socially adept creatures and love to work, simply for the social aspect of it. They don't enjoy working alone and do best in partnerships, groups, or in some sort of a collaborative process. These folks prefer harmony and balance in their workplace and are drawn to careers that create this dynamic for others. They can get caught up in their attempts to please everyone, and this can occasionally make them appear indecisive. This sign tends to steer clear of arguments and bring a calming presence to their workplace, striving for equality and fairness always. Libras enjoy using their ambition toward intellectual pursuits. Careers tailored for this sign include therapist, counselor, mediator, attorney, matchmaker, negotiator, manager, event planner, musician, DJ, liberal arts professor, and business administrator.

Scorpio

Powerhouses to the core, Scorpios are hard driving and dedicated to their passion projects and purpose work, if you leave them to do things their way. Working solo is best for this sign, as they are known for their occasional temper flares. Their discreet and secretive nature means they are often misunderstood by their peers. In general, they are diligent and deeply in tune with the psyche of the office dynamics and coworkers. Scorpios are poised, self-motivated, and resourceful. Ideal jobs for Scorpios are ones in which they can play to their deeply obsessive core. Jobs that are good fits include psychotherapy, researcher, forensics, market analysist, copy editor, film editor, marketing, graphic design, investigator, political analyst, sex therapist or coach, dominatrix, shamanic healer, or boudoir photographer.

Sagittarius

Curious and upbeat, Sagittarius possesses a high degree of independence and individualism, often going off abruptly in their own direction. This sign is intuitive, hardworking, energetic, and versatile, but may come across as impulsive at times. Working in group dynamics to gain knowledge is often best for Sagittarius, before stepping out on their own in projects and endeavors. Once they feel comfortable with the material, they are able to make quick decisions and pivot accordingly, producing undeniable results over time. They are normally the fun, cool bosses or coworkers, and will most certainly be using all their vacation days. Positions ideal for Sagittarius are travel blogger or guide, yoga teacher, college professor, journalist, publisher, interpreter, attorney, judge, hospitalist, hotel manager, entrepreneur, architect, personal trainer, and brand ambassador.

Capricorn

Capricorn is most interested in creating something solid and lasting. They are hardworking, persistent souls with ambition. Often this sign will want to work without taking orders and without question. You'll find lots of Capricorns in top-level management positions within companies. They don't make much fuss or drama and are best suited to an environment that supports their strong work ethic. Focus is the name of their game, and there is no one better to handle crisis situations or manage a difficult team member than

Capricorn. Businesslike and reserved, this sign often follows the rules to a T. Jobs for Capricorns include CEO, CPA, physician, financial planner, business manager, legal secretary, paralegal, dentist, supply chain manager, graphic designer, and analyst.

Aquarius

Aquarians are great morale builders for any team, though they prefer not to take orders from others when they are immersed in their own process. This sign's personality is witty and fun to be around, so there's never a dull moment working around them. They feel most fulfilled when their time and energy is working toward the greatest good of the community and thrive when they can champion a good cause. As nonconformists, Aquarians will make their own rules and create new pathways for others to follow. Typical of air signs, Aquarians may come across as absentminded or forgetful and do not work well on timelines. Great jobs for Aquarians include marine biologist, astrologer, healer, environmental planner, activist, life coach, artist, entrepreneur, social worker, musician, writer, or hypnotherapist.

Pisces

These creative visionaries lead others in a soft and gentle manner. It's important for them to find a career that aligns with their sensitive soul, away from noisy and hectic environments. This sign is a dutiful worker in the right calm setting, and they prefer to flow from task to task creatively and in a manner that suits their mood. Cookie-cutter jobs in the corporate world aren't for them, as they prefer living in the abstract. They do make wonderful coworkers, though, because of their selflessness and flexibility. Adaptable and empathetic, you can turn to them as a shoulder to cry on anytime. Great jobs for Pisces include artist, therapist, musician, energy healer, astrologer, dancer, social worker, interior decorator, writer, actor, and guidance counselor.

Key Takeaways

This chapter presented you with information about how each sign is best suited in a working environment and what kind of traits are expressed under each cosmic blueprint. Let's quickly recap some of the things covered in chapter 10.

◆ The tenth and sixth houses hold important information about your purpose work, as well as your north and south node points in your birth chart.

◆ The midheaven, MC point, is the highest place on your chart, giving you a glimpse of your highest expression and soul strategy.

◆ Eclipses are dynamic cosmic occurrences involving the sun, moon, and earth that can shift realities and cause transformational processes to activate.

◆ Stay open to possibilities as you work with the suggestions in this chapter to enhance your natural abilities and direct yourself toward optimal career opportunities.

A Final Word

Congratulations for taking an important step on your astrological journey by reading this book! You now have the tools to begin performing basic readings and interpret your own findings to help assist you in your personal expansion. Astrology is rich in symbolism and can represent an entire life's work. To have the know-how to read the finer details of someone's birth chart, you'll want to continue practicing. This is the most valuable piece of advice I can give, because there is no replacement for time spent doing the work. Remember to be patient with yourself while you are building your skills, as this takes time. In this case, it's perfectly acceptable to start with the basics (sun, moon, rising) and stay there until you are ready to move on to reading more intricate aspects of a natal chart (like current transits, conjunctions, aspects, and planetary placements).

Your new tools equip you to better understand yourself and improve your life from the inside out. As always, allow your intuition to guide you. Take what resonates and leave the rest. If something doesn't make sense, set it aside and pick it back up later. As with all things, you work best when you unplug for a little. Sharing your new practice with friends is one way you can ensure you get plenty of practice in. Above all else, remember to have fun. May the long-time sun guide shine upon you, and may you always know what a precious gift you are to this Universe.

10 Commonly Asked Questions, Answered

Now that you have had practice with the basics and have some suggestions to get you going on your celestial path, you will be able to start to understand the relationships between the signs, elements, modalities, aspects, and planets. If you wish to truly harness all that astrology has to offer, make sure you continue practicing and sharing your journey. Over time, these components will become second nature and working with them will feel fulfilling as your confidence increases and you expand your knowledge.

The following section helps answer some common questions that pop up when you are launching your journey through astrology. It is my hope that you'll be able to learn the intricacies of your own simple birth chart before moving on to more advanced chart details, like aspect analysis and transits. This craft takes a lifetime of work to practice and study completely, as there are multiple systems and schools of thought within systems. As you continue your journey, take things in stride, and embrace where you are in your process. You are always growing and learning, and there's no better time to use this information for your own progression and growth.

I've heard Mercury retrograde is often a stressful time for people. How do I know how it will affect me by reading my chart?

Mercury's inauspicious effects have been known to disrupt the field a bit when Mercury is in retrograde. Retrograde is a time when the planet's energies turn inward. It's easy to see how Mercury is going to affect you when it comes around. First, check to see what sign Mercury will be in when it turns retrograde. This will inform you about what energies will be in play during the retrograde. Then you'll want to look at your birth chart to see if Mercury was direct when you were born. You can use a free retrograde calculator online to obtain this. If it was in retrograde, you'll likely fare much better naturally during these times.

How do I find the best time to make a big decision this month?

You would want to start by looking up the next Mercury retrograde (Rx) dates. During Mercury Rx, communication and technology typically breaks down and you are advised not to launch into new projects, sign any important documents, or make any big decisions. Typically, these occur two to six times a year, so make sure your big decision making falls outside of any retrogrades to ensure success. In addition, it's advised not to make any big decisions around the new moon because this is a time for resetting and can leave you feeling confused and disoriented. Looking at where Jupiter is transiting in your chart can also give you an idea of the timing of major opportunities. For example, you'd want to see it in the tenth house if you were waiting on a career move.

What if I don't know my exact time of birth?

You will be unable to distill exact moon or rising signs without a specific time and place of birth, but you can still work with your sun sign. Many astrology clocks will come close if you enter 12:00 p.m. for your birth chart if you do not know your exact time of birth.

How does the Vedic system of astrology compare with the tropical system used in this book?

Vedic astrology, or Hindu astrology, contains rich culture as well as ancient astrology dating back to 10,000 BCE. Like modern Western astrology, it serves as a guide and road map to help understand the human experience. However, Vedic astrology uses the sidereal calendar for zodiac calculations, and Western astrology uses the tropical calendar. Because the calendars are different, the signs run to different parts of the month, and your signs may be different from what you're used to under a Vedic context. The information in this book is based on the Western (tropical) astrology, though if you know your Vedic chart, you may adapt the practices and use them accordingly.

If my natal chart is like the blueprint for my life, how much of life is fate vs. free will?

You live on Earth, which is the planet of free will. You always have a choice in how you show up in the world. Although there are several ways your "coding" can play out in your lifetime, you also have choices every day to use your free will, which essentially allows you to evolve past your own limitations. Signs, planets, aspects, and transits will show you what you are working with, but what they won't show you is what you are going to choose to do with that information. There are so many ways your chart can work for you, that just one destiny simply doesn't exist. Living is about the journey, not the destination.

What is one of the top benefits of studying astrology?

I believe astrology allows you to become instantaneously more understanding of those around you, especially those who you've had conflict with. By embracing someone's nature, you can build resilience and patience when you accept their design. Everyone has their own strengths and weaknesses, and astrology is made to point those things out. Astrology can be used to schedule important decisions in life as a predictive tool. Overall, it can highlight when to do or not do something, and that can be very valuable information if used correctly.

Can astrology and religion coexist?

Absolutely! In fact, many people report spiritual awakenings and revelations after they have started working with their astrology. Astrology doesn't hold any religious undertones, but instead helps you build your consciousness, mapping an order to the Universe at large. With this information, you can lean into your purpose work, strengths, and passions in life. Religion won't interfere, and astrology shouldn't be confused as a tool for worship. Astrologists are geared toward using psychology and intuition, instead of divination to read your horoscope. The way you look at the stars and how they relate to timing and events on earth can be considered synchronistic.

Should I date somebody if our sun sign/synastry chart isn't compatible?

When looking at synastry charts, there are energies that go well together and some that do not. When answering this question, think about all the times you've met somebody who has appeared one way on paper, but the chemistry just wasn't there in reality (and vice versa). Charts should be used to give you an idea of your ideal match, but nothing in astrology is predetermined or destined. Optimal matches exist, and depending on how much work someone has done, they may have learned to rise above the issues that may show up as incompatible within a chart. When considering giving someone a chance, throw away any limiting ideas that their astrological sign needs to be your ideal match.

Are horoscopes that I read in the papers the same as astrology?

Proper astrology readings get a bad rap, mostly from these horoscopes written for papers and articles as gimmicky clickbait. It's impossible to forecast an entire sign's qualities (that covers the scope of millions of people worldwide) in a few sentences accurately. If you think about it this way, it's just not reasonable to lump everyone into categories like that. That kind of horoscope was created to appeal to mass audiences and not individuals. Real readings with accurate information combine data from a wide range of sources and base the information on points, planets, and transits. Though horoscope write-ups can be entertaining, it would be unwise to follow these as a basis for direction or prediction of any kind. By pulling your own chart and looking at current transits, you'll get a better idea of what to expect in the coming days, week, and months ahead.

Is astrology a pseudoscience?

Though astrology isn't fake, it has had its moments of scientific scrutiny. As with all realms of spirituality and belief, there will always be those who prefer to diminish and condemn the modality because of their own inability to connect to their spiritual side. Additionally, modern astrology has close ties to the social science of pop psychology and has suffered because of its reputation as a trend or fad. However, traditional astrology is derived from astronomy, an observational science. You need only to open your mind to begin to welcome in new insights that can be available to you when you ditch the need for everything to fit into a perfect box or category. My advice is if astrology is helpful to you, don't bother defending it to those without ears to hear.

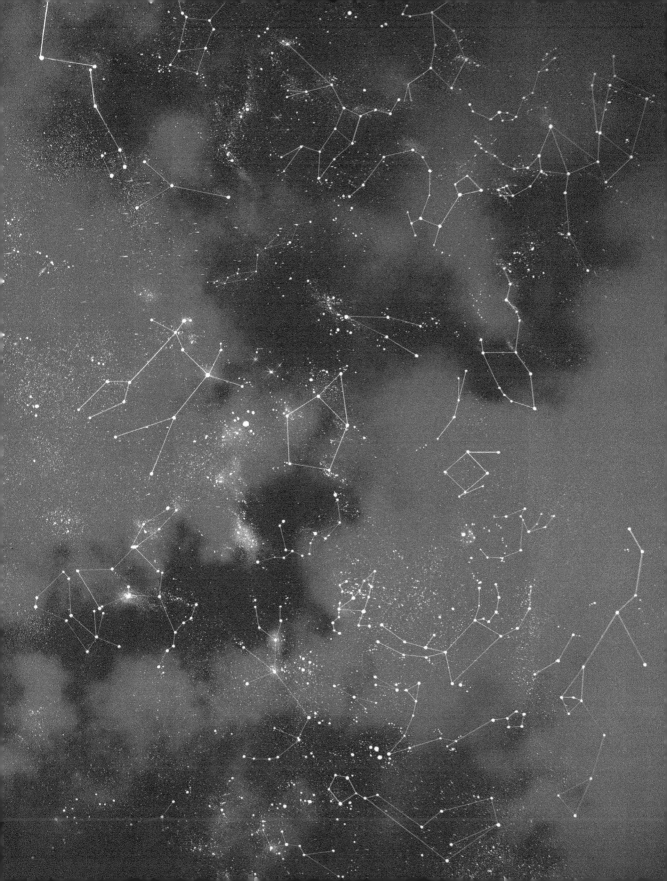

Glossary

Angles: In a birth chart, these are the lines that divide your chart vertically and horizontally. They are the ascendant, descendant, midheaven, and Imum Coeli. These points tell you more about various aspects of your personality.

Archetype: As defined by Carl Jung, these are universal models that serve to represent the collective subconscious. The twelve archetypes are the Innocent, Everyman, Hero, Outlaw, Explorer, Creator, Ruler, Magician, Lover, Caregiver, Jester, and Sage. These can be found within a birth chart in the planets and signs.

Ascendant: This is another term for your rising sign, this point of your birth chart shows the sign that was in the sky on the eastern horizon at the time of your birth. This represents an integration of all aspects of your chart, and some systems believe it to be the most important part of your personal astrology.

Aspect: When two or more planets line up in the sky at certain angles, this is known as aspecting each other. The energies may mix and mingle, creating various harmonies or disharmonic effects.

Big Three: Your sun, moon, and rising (ascendant) sign make up your Big Three in astrology. These primary astrology signs rule over certain areas of your life. For example, the sun is your outward personality, the moon is your inner personality, and your rising sign is the mask you wear around others.

Birth Chart: An astrological chart representing the positions of planets in the zodiac at the time of your birth. This is also known as a natal chart, and knowing the time, place, and location of your birth is necessary to obtain your exact zodiac placements.

Conjunction: This is when two or more planets form a close connection under a sign. This combination of energy serves to intensify the effects of the planets.

Cusp: This is the dividing line between two houses or signs in the zodiac. If you were born the day of a transitional period between signs, you are said to be born on the cusp and can carry traits of both or either sign.

Element: A pure natural substance that cannot be broken down into anything else. The five elements in nature are fire, earth, air, water, and ether.

Ether: Known as the fifth element, ether is a nonmaterial substance that fills the entire Universe. It is neither sky nor gas, but rather an essence of consciousness.

Glyphs: These are symbols that represent the signs and planets in a birth chart.

Horoscope: This can refer to either a short forecast of your sign within a newspaper or editorial piece, or an actual birth chart containing information from your personal zodiac.

Luminary: A natural, light-giving body, such as the sun or moon.

Lunar Phases: The phases of the moon. There are four major phases and four transition phases. These are new, waxing crescent, first quarter, waxing gibbous, full, waning gibbous, third quarter, and waning crescent.

Midheaven (MC): An angle in a birth chart at the cusp of the tenth house, representing the soul's passion and purpose work in one's lifetime.

Nodes: The north and south nodes of the moon in a birth chart represent the two points where the moon's orbit intersects with the ecliptic. The moon crosses in a northerly direction (dharma point) and then a southernly directly (karma point), creating the nodes from an earthly perspective.

Reiki: A gentle form of energy work that involves either hands-on healing or remote distance healing. *Rei* means Universal, and *ki* means energy.

Stellium: When three or more planets are present in one house or sign in a birth chart a stellium is created, giving concentration or emphasis to that area of your chart.

Synastry: A synastry chart compares the relationships of two people by layering their individual charts on top of one another. You can then compare certain markers between the charts to assess compatibility.

Transit: When a planet moves in the sky, this is called a transit. It may be moving into a new zodiac house or sign or going retrograde.

Tropical Zodiac: The tropical zodiac is the zodiac most used by Westerners in astrology. The relationship of the earth and the sun based on the seasons is what is known as the tropical zodiac.

Yin/Yang: Yin and yang are feminine and masculine energies, respectively. They should not be confused for gender. Rather, they represent the polarities of energy present in everyone of every sex.

Resources

Books

Goldschneider, Gary. *The Astrology of You and Me: How to Understand and Improve Every Relationship in Your Life*. Philadelphia, PA: Quirk Books, 2018. Snarky and entertaining, Gary weighs in on how to manage every relationship in your life, depending on your (and their) personal astrology.

Edut, Ophira, and Tali Edut. *The AstroTwins' 2022 Horoscope: The Complete Yearly Astrology Guide for Every Zodiac Sign*. Astrostyle publishing by Simon & Schuster, New York: Atria Books, December 17, 2021. Accurate horoscopes for the year ahead, updated annually.

Edington, Louise. *The Complete Guide to Astrology: Understanding Yourself, Your Signs, and Your Birth Chart*. Emeryville, California: Rockridge Press, 2020. In-depth definitions and beyond-the-basics information for people looking to deepen their relationship with the planets and astrology.

Askinosie, Heather, and Timmi Jandro. *Crystal Muse: Everyday Rituals to Tune into the Real You*. San Diego: Hay House, June 12, 2018. Rituals and crystal practices to enhance your understanding and abilities in working with crystal energy from two old-school crystal experts.

Freed, Jennifer, PhD. *Use Your Planets Wisely: Master Your Ultimate Potential with Psychological Astrology*. Boulder, Colorado: Sounds True Publishing, 2020. A practical guide to evolving through your personal astrology.

Podcast

The Rising Sign Podcast with Colin Bedell. Colin gives his entertaining outlooks on all things astrology and explains in a practical, no-nonsense way how celestial events impact our daily lives.

Websites

David Palmer: Theleoking.com. David is an incredibly gifted astrologer and TV personality with entertaining forecasts on current events and astrological happenings.

Magic of I Website: Magicofi.com. Kerry gives you a chance to follow along with daily astrology planners with current transits for each day of the year. Moon cycles are included along with a mini training key to help you on your cosmic journey.

Sloan Bella: Sloanbella.com. Meet Sloan, an incredibly gifted astrologer and psychic medium from Los Angeles. Follow her on YouTube for astrology readings and more.

References

Edut, Ophira, and Tali Edut. "The 12 Houses of the Zodiac." Astrostyle.com. March 10, 2021. astrostyle.com/learn-astrology/the-12-zodiac-houses.

Kahn, Nina. "The Modalities in Astrology Say So Much About Your Personality." Bustle.com. August 16, 2021. bustle.com/life/is-your-zodiac-sign-cardinal -fixed-mutable-heres-what-it-all-means-19418010.

Keen Editorial Staff. "3 Different Types of Astrology You Should Know." Keen.com. January 11, 2021. keen.com/articles/astrology/3-different-types-of-astrology -you-should-know.

Magliochetti, Michaela. "Zodiac Planets, Explained. What Each Celestial Body Says About You." Purewow.com. November 11, 2020. purewow.com/wellness/ zodiac-planets.

Owings, Shannon. "The 12 Literary Archetypes." Medium.com. April 3, 2020. medium.com/the-brave-writer/the-12-literary-archetypes-1e623ac06ca5.

Randell, Brooke. "24 Gemstones Meanings: The Surprising Symbolism of Your Jewels." BrilliantEarth.com. October 8, 2021. brilliantearth.com/news/ gemstone-meanings-the-surprising-symbolism-of-your-jewels.

Waxman, Olivia. "Where Do Zodiac Signs Come From?" Time.com. June 21, 2018. time.com/5315377/are-zodiac-signs-real-astrology-history.

Index

Acknowledgments

As always, I'd like to thank my beloved partner, Will, for supporting and encouraging me in all ways possible. I love you. Thank you to our kids, who aren't old enough to read yet but will someday, hopefully, read this to me.

Thank you to my friends and family for your understanding, love, and support. To my fellow astrologists, thank you for leading the way for others to build upon this sacred practice.

Thank you to Kristen, who first introduced me to *Love Signs* by Linda Goodman, an everlasting classic that spawned my curiosity into astrology.

I offer deep gratitude to my students, who inspire me, always proving that reality is illustrious and multidimensional.

Last but not least, thank you to Skyla the Frenchie, my beloved dog daughter, who is nine years old now.

About the Author

 **April Pfender** is the founder of Golden Light Alchemy, providing a healing focus that combines her years of trauma-informed healing with Reiki and other various healing modalities. April is a Reiki master teacher, quantum healing facilitator, sound healer, and meditation instructor who has been studying, teaching, and writing about self-empowerment in recent years. Her other books are *Chakra Balance*, *Essential Chakra Meditation*, *The Complete Guide to Chakras*, *Reiki Healing for the Chakras*, and *Crystal Zodiac for Beginners*. Her work has carried her through a deeply spiritual journey, enabling her to help people through their own healing and ascension journeys at this time.

April is a daughter, a mother, a lover, a healer, a way shower, and a teacher to many. She currently resides on the East Coast with her beloved partner and hosts virtual and in-person training classes as well as retreats.

Printed in the USA
CPSIA information can be obtained
at www.ICGtesting.com
LVHW061128290424
778214LV00003B/10